SOUP SEASON

SOUP SEASON

OVER 70 RECIPES FOR SOUPS, PLUS SIDES & TOPPINGS TO MATCH

HANNAH MILES

RYLAND PETERS & SMALL

DEDICATION

For beautiful Katie and Elsie, with love xxx

Designer Paul Stradling
Production Manager Gordana Simakovic
Creative Director Leslie Harrington
Editorial Director Julia Charles

Food stylists Octavia Squire, Ellie Tarn & Lucy McKelvie
Prop stylists Luis Peral & Steve Painter

Indexer Hilary Bird

This edition published in 2026 by
Ryland Peters & Small
20–21 Jockey's Fields
London WC1R 4BW
www.rylandpeters.com
email: euregulations@rylandpeters.com

First published in 2022 as *A Bowl of Soup*. Some recipes in this book were also previously published in *Soup & a Sandwich* by Hannah Miles in 2016.

ISBN: 978-1-78879-774-0

10 9 8 7 6 5 4 3 2 1

Printed and bound in China.

MIX
Paper | Supporting responsible forestry
FSC www.fsc.org FSC® C008047

NOTES

- Both British (Metric) and American (Imperial plus US cup measurements) are included in these recipes for your convenience; however it is important to work with one set of measurements and not alternate between the two within a recipe.
- All spoon measurements are level unless otherwise specified. 1 teaspoon = 5 ml, 1 tablespoon = 15 ml.
- When a recipe calls for the grated zest of citrus fruit, buy unwaxed fruit and wash well before using. If you can only find treated fruit, scrub well in warm soapy water before using.
- Ovens should be preheated to the specified temperatures. If using a fan-assisted oven, adjust temperatures according to the manufacturer's instructions.

A CIP record for this book is available from the British Library.

US Library of Congress CIP data has been applied for.

The authorised representative in the EEA is
Authorised Rep Compliance Ltd.,
Ground Floor, 71 Lower Baggot Street,

CONTENTS

INTRODUCTION

Soups are one of the easiest and most satisfying meals – with just a few ingredients you can whip up a tasty bowl in only a matter of minutes. There are endless possibilities for soup combinations so whatever your favourite ingredient there is sure to be a soup in this book for you. Soups are perfect prepare-ahead meals as they can be made the day before and stored in the refrigerator, or for the more organized can be frozen ahead (see the guide to freezing on page 7, opposite.)

The *Classic Soups* chapter contains those much-loved family favourite recipes – tomato soup, French onion, creamy chicken soup and rich minestrone as well as smoked cullen skink and flavours of India with a spiced lentil soup and curried parsnip soup. For a luxurious treat there is also fresh asparagus soup with a poached egg garnish. *Satisfying Soups* brings you the heartiest of soups – pearl barley broth with lamb, sausage and cabbage soup and for winter days a Brussels and chestnut soup with bacon whilst *Soups for the Soul* are those go to soups for a pick me up – the classic Jewish "penicillin" of chicken and matzo ball soup (my go-to broth when I am under the weather) or a buttery baked potato soup laced with cheese and cream. The *Soups for Summer* chapter contains light soups for summer days – with refreshing citrus flavours of a zucchini lemon and yogurt soup, sweetcorn lime and chilli/chile soup and my personal favourite avgolemono (Greek chicken soup with rice and lemon). This chapter also contains a delicious array of chilled soups – perfect for summer *al fresco* dining in the sun – with chilled ajo blanco – a wonderful Spanish garlic, almond and vinegar soup – strawberry gazpacho and chilled broad/fava bean, pea and mint soup.

For more quirky flavours the *Something Special* chapter will tingle your taste buds – cheese and beer soup, Caribbean-style sweet potato and coconut soup and an earthy aubergine/eggplant, chilli/chile and tomato soup. For a bit of glamour there is an egg ribbon soup is topped with caviar and gold leaf. The *Soup and a Sandwich* chapter contains complete meals and perfect pairings of broth and dippers to match – prawn/shrimp saganaki pittas to pair with red (bell) pepper fennel and ouzo soup, garlic mushroom soup with bresaola focaccia or even miso soup with a sushi sandwich. For adding texture and interest to your soups, *Garnishes and Toppings* (see pages 10–15) provides recipes for croûtons, savoury granola, truffle seed mix and crispy onions as well as drizzles, from homemade pesto to flavoured oils. *Breads* contains accompaniments for soups, from traditional buttermilk biscuits, popovers, a useful gluten-free cornbread and savoury muffins. The recipes in this book will feed hungry tummies whatever the weather or occasion. Start your soup adventure today!

GUIDE TO SOUP MAKING

The key steps to soup making are:

• Use the best, freshest ingredients you can get. Always use vegetables when they are in season as this will give the best taste.

• Take time to prepare the soup base – don't rush caramelizing the onions or sweating down vegetables. Do this slowly over a gentle heat as this will allow maximum flavours to develop.

• When blending soups, for best results you need a powerful blender, food processor or blending stick. Using a high-power blender will ensure that the soup is very smooth.

• For the smoothest of soups, once blended you can pass your soup through a moulin or a fine-mesh sieve/strainer, pressing through with a rubber spatula. This will leave behind any small pieces of vegetable skins and will give you the best results.

• Most soups keep well in the refrigerator for a few days so they can be prepared ahead and just reheated when you want to serve.

SHORT CUTS FOR SOUP-MAKING

• If you are making soup, you can easily double-batch the recipe and freeze the second half in individual portions so that they can be defrosted for super quick standby lunches or suppers.

• When making stock make a double-batch and freeze half for later as this saves time.

• Whilst making your own stock is definitely worthwhile (see pages 8–9) supermarkets and delicatessens have a wide range of good ready-made stocks or stock pots that you dissolve in water. Using these can save you time.

• There are no real hard and fast rules when making soups so if you are missing a certain vegetable, it is often no problem to substitute it with another.

• To add extra flourish to soups, serve with a variety of sprinkles and toppings – there are ideas on pages 10–15. Adding crunchy croûtons or savoury granola will add another texture dimension to your soups.

FREEZING SOUPS

• Most soups recipes in the book can be frozen, with a few exceptions. Fish soups do not freeze well but you can make the liquid base of the recipe ahead and freeze it and then when you are ready to serve, just defrost and cook the fish following the remaining steps in the recipe. Similarly for soups that contain cream or eggs, prepare the recipe to the stage before adding the cream or egg and freeze. Once defrosted reheat the soup and add the cream or egg at that stage.

• There are a wide variety of freezer tubs and freezer bags that are designed for storing soups. My brother likes to pour soup into bags and then lay them flat on a baking tray to freeze so that your soup freezes in a flat layer. Once frozen remove the baking tray and then the soups can be easily stacked in layers in your freezer to save space.

• Make sure that you taste the soup for seasoning on reheating after freezing as the freezing process can adjust the seasoning.

• Label your soups clearly as to what they are and the date of freezing. Soups should be eaten within 3 months of freezing.

BASIC STOCKS

VEGETABLE STOCK

Vegetable stock is perfect for making vegetarian soups. This is my base stock, but you can add additional vegetables if you have some to use up. You can also change the herbs – such as using basil and rosemary for tomato-based soups or coriander/cilantro for Asian-flavoured stock.

1 tablespoon olive oil
2 carrots, peeled and finely chopped
1 onion, sliced
1 leek, sliced
2 sticks/ribs celery, finely sliced
10 peppercorns
1 bouquet garni

In a large saucepan over a gentle heat, heat the olive oil and add the chopped carrots, onion, leek and celery and cook until the onion is soft and translucent, and the leek is soft. Add about 2 litres/8 cups of water and simmer for about 30 minutes until the liquid has reduced by half.

Strain through a fine-mesh sieve/strainer, ideally lined with muslin/cheesecloth to remove any impurities.

Allow to cool then transfer into a lidded tub and store in the refrigerator until you are ready to use, or freeze until needed.

CHICKEN STOCK

It is worth the effort to make your own chicken stock as it really does have a better flavour than store-bought. Use the carcass from a roast dinner or, if you are making a soup that calls for chicken, use a whole chicken in place of the carcass, then remove the cooked chicken to add back into the soup.

1 chicken carcass
2 carrots, peeled and sliced
2 sticks/ribs celery, sliced
1 onion, sliced
1 teaspoon peppercorns
1 bouquet garni
salt

Place the carcass and any left-over chicken in a large stock pot with the carrots, celery, onion, peppercorns bouquet garni and salt. Fill the pan with water and simmer for about 1½–2 hours until the water has reduced by half.

Skim away any froth on top of the broth and then strain through a fine-mesh sieve/strainer, ideally lined with muslin/cheesecloth to remove any impurities. Discard the bones and vegetables.

Once cooled, store the stock in the refrigerator overnight. The following day remove any fat that has set on top of the stock. If you are freezing the stock, do so after you have removed any set fat.

MEAT STOCK

A rich beef soup needs a good stock. Good butchers will have beef bones for sale, or often for free, and although the stock takes a good many hours to prepare, it is worth taking the time for a really good flavour.

about 2 kg/2 lb. 4 oz. beef bones
2 large onions, cut into wedges
3 garlic cloves
3 carrots, peeled and cut into large chunks
2 leeks, cut into chunks
2 sticks/ribs celery, sliced
2 large tomatoes, halved
1 teaspoon peppercorns
1 bouquet garni
salt

Preheat the oven to 180°C (350 °F) Gas 4.

Place the bones, onions, garlic, carrots and leeks in a large roasting pan and roast in the preheated oven for around 40–50 minutes until the bones turn brown. Baste from time to time during cooking.

Tip the bones and vegetables into a large stock pot and cover with water. Add the tomatoes, peppercorns, bouquet garni and a little salt and simmer over a gentle heat for 3–4 hours. Add more salt to taste.

Skim away any froth on top and then strain through a fine-mesh sieve/strainer, ideally lined with muslin/cheesecloth to remove any impurities. Discard the bones and vegetables. Once cooled, store the stock in the refrigerator overnight. The following day remove any fat that has set on top. If you are freezing it, do so after you have removed any set fat.

FISH STOCK

This stock does not take long to prepare and is rich with the flavour of prawns/shrimp. You can also use lobster shells, if you like. If you do not want to include shellfish, just use fish bones for a lighter stock.

1 tablespoon olive oil
shells and heads of prawns/shrimp and fish bones
2 carrots, peeled and finely chopped
1 large onion, finely chopped
1 stick/rib celery, finely chopped
½ bulb fennel, finely chopped
250 ml/1 cup white wine
3 tomatoes
2 teaspoons tomato purée/paste
1 teaspoon peppercorns
1 bouquet garni
salt

In a large stock pot, heat the olive oil and add the prawn/shrimp shells and heads and fish bones, and cook for 5–10 minutes until the shells turn pink. Press down on the shells and bones with a potato masher to release the juices. Add the carrots, onion, celery and fennel and sauté for 15 minutes over a gentle heat until the onion is soft and translucent.

Add the white wine and simmer for a few minutes to burn off the alcohol. Fill the pan with water so that all the bones and shells are covered and simmer for about 30 minutes, adding in the tomatoes, tomato purée/paste, peppercorns and bouquet garni, pressing down with a masher from time to time to release the flavour.

Strain through a fine-mesh sieve/strainer, ideally lined with muslin/cheesecloth to remove any impurities and season with salt to taste. Leave to cool, then chill in the refrigerator for up to 3 days before using, or freeze until needed.

GARNISHES & TOPPINGS

GARLIC CROUTONS

Croutons are one of the most traditional toppings for a soup. You can buy them ready made from the supermarket, but this recipe is super easy and always popular. Who doesn't like crisp fried bread!

2 sprigs of fresh rosemary
4 slices of bread, crusts removed (stale bread is fine)
2 garlic cloves (there is no need to remove the skin)
olive oil, for drizzling
salt and pepper

Preheat the oven to 180°C (350°F) Gas 4.

Place the rosemary, bread and garlic in a roasting pan and drizzle with olive oil so that the bread is lightly coated in the oil. Toss the bread with a spoon so that it is coated all over. Season with salt and pepper.

Bake in the preheated oven for about 10 minutes until lightly golden brown and crisp. Remove the rosemary and garlic before serving.

PANGRATTATO

Translating as 'breadcrumbs', pangrattato is often referred to as poor man's Parmesan. However, it definitely doesn't taste like a poor man's version of anything when sprinkled onto soup.

1 slice of dried bread
olive oil, for drizzling
salt and pepper

Blitz the bread to fine crumbs in a food processor.

Heat a little olive oil in a frying pan/skillet and add the crumbs. Season with salt and pepper and toast until the breadcrumbs are crisp. Stir all the time to make sure that the crumbs don't burn.

Variations: You can vary this recipe by adding a peeled clove of garlic or some lemon zest to the blender when processing the crumbs, or you can fry small bacon pieces at the same time as the crumbs.

WELSH RAREBIT TOASTS

Welsh rarebit is a traditional English farmhouse dish. It can be made in many ways depending on the region – for example some people add beer or ale to it. It is a gooey cheesy delight and goes well with many soups.

80 g/scant 1 cup grated Cheddar
1 large/extra large egg
1 teaspoon wholegrain mustard
a good dash of Worcestershire sauce
small squares of bread
salt and pepper

In a bowl, whisk together the cheese, egg, mustard and Worcestershire sauce and season with salt and pepper.

Place the breads under a hot grill/broiler and lightly toast on both sides. Place a small spoonful of the cheese mix on top of each bread and grill/broil until golden brown.

Add a small splash of Worcestershire sauce to each and serve warm.

CRISPY ONIONS

One of the simplest toppings for a soup is some crispy onions – they add flavour and texture, and keep well stored in an airtight jar for a week.

3 tablespoons ghee or clarified butter
1 small red onion, finely sliced
salt and pepper

Heat the ghee in a pan until hot, then add the onion and stir regularly until the onion is crisp and golden brown.

Remove from the oil with a slotted spoon and drain on paper towels. Season with salt and pepper.

SAVOURY GRANOLA

A sprinkling of this savoury, crunchy granola will liven up all sorts of soups, as well as adding a pleasing crunch. Adjust the quantity of chilli/chili powder to your liking.

150 g/1½ cups rolled/ old-fashioned oats
70 g/½ cup pine nuts
50 g/⅜ cup sunflower seeds
50 g/⅓ cup pumpkin seeds/ pepitas
20 g/2 tablespoons sesame seeds
1 tablespoon olive oil
2 tablespoons pure maple syrup
1 tablespoon soy sauce
½–1 teaspoon chilli/chili powder, to taste
30 g/scant ½ cup finely grated Parmesan
salt and pepper

Preheat the oven to 150°C (300°F) Gas 2.

Place all of the ingredients in a mixing bowl and stir well so that everything is mixed. Pour onto the lined baking sheet and bake in the preheated oven for 45 minutes until crisp, turning several times throughout cooking so that it is evenly cooked and does not burn.

Test for seasoning and add a little more salt if needed – it is best to add this at the end, as the soy sauce will add saltiness to the granola.

TOASTED TRUFFLE SEED MIX

A simple mix of seeds with the added flavour of truffle. A spoonful of these seeds adds flavour, texture and some extra nutrition to soups.

3 tablespoons sunflower seeds
3 tablespoons pumpkin seeds
3 tablespoons sesame seeds
1 teaspoon truffle salt
black pepper

Place all of the seeds in a dry frying pan/skillet together with the truffle salt and pepper. Stir with a spatula for a few minutes over the heat until the sunflower seeds turn light golden brown. Take care that they do not burn, and tip out from the pan as soon as you have finished cooking.

Allow to cool, then store in an airtight jar.

FLAVOURED OILS

Flavoured oils are ideal for drizzling over soups to add a little garnish and extra flavour. There are a lot of flavoured oils available in supermarkets. If you want to try your own, you will need a sterilized bottle, olive oil (I like to use extra virgin, but a mild olive oil also works well) and flavourings such as slices of garlic, fresh rosemary, dried basil, sliced fresh chillies/chiles or strips of lemon rind or orange rind. Place your chosen flavourings into the sterilized bottle and pour over the oil until the bottle is full. It is important that your flavourings are fully submerged to prevent mould forming on the top of the oil. Use within a few weeks and store in a dark place.

FRESH HERB MIX

Fresh herbs have a wonderful fragrance and scent, and they are delicious sprinkled on top of soups. You can use any combination of herbs you like, such as basil, mint, oregano, coriander/cilantro, chives and dill. Finely chop the herbs and sprinkle them on to your soup, or mix them with a drizzle of olive oil, a squeeze of lemon or lime juice (depending on the flavour of your soup) and salt and pepper to make a herb drizzle.

AVOCADO CREAM

Creamy, flavourful and luxurious, avocado cream is quick to make and can be spooned onto the top of many soups.

1 ripe avocado, pitted and peeled
freshly squeezed juice of ½ lemon
150 ml/⅔ cup double/heavy cream
salt and pepper

Put the avocado flesh into a mixing bowl with the lemon juice and whisk them together until smooth using an electric hand-hand whisk. It is important to use a ripe avocado so that the cream is not bitter.

Pour in the double/heavy cream and whisk until the mixture thickens. Season with salt and pepper.

HOMEMADE PESTO

Fresh pesto makes a great drizzle on many soups, particularly tomato soup.

2 handfuls of fresh basil leaves
3 tablespoons toasted pine nuts or pistachios
1 garlic clove
3 tablespoons olive oil
3 tablespoons freshly grated Parmesan
salt and pepper

Place the basil and pine nuts or pistachios in a large pestle and mortar with the garlic clove and crush to a smooth paste. Add the oil gradually, together with the Parmesan, salt and pepper, and grind together until you have a smooth paste.

Store the pesto in the refrigerator for 2–3 days in a sterilized jar with a layer of olive oil on top.

If you want to make a truffle-flavoured pesto, add a little truffle oil or truffle salt to the mixture.

CHAPTER 1

CLASSIC SOUPS

ROASTED TOMATO SOUP WITH PESTO DRIZZLE

Sometimes a soup can have very few ingredients but still be bursting with flavour. Here roasting the tomatoes with a sprinkling of salt and a drizzle of balsamic vinegar gives them a real zing. Serve with a simple pesto drizzle and a panini on the side, if you like.

700 g/1½ lb. cherry tomatoes
olive oil, to drizzle
1 tablespoon balsamic glaze or vinegar
1 teaspoon caster/granulated sugar
800 ml/generous 3¼ cups vegetable stock
150 ml/⅔ cup single/light cream
a handful of fresh basil
salt and pepper
pesto, store-bought or homemade (see page 15), to drizzle
panini of your choice, to serve (optional)

SERVES 4

Preheat the oven to 180°C (350°F) Gas 4.

Place the tomatoes in a roasting pan. Drizzle over the olive oil and balsamic glaze or vinegar, sprinkle with the sugar and season well with salt and pepper. Shake the pan well so all the tomatoes are coated. Roast for 20–30 minutes until the tomatoes are soft.

Place the tomatoes and the roasting liquid from the pan into a saucepan and add the stock. Simmer over a low heat for 15 minutes, and then place in a blender or food processor and blitz until very smooth, or use a stick blender.

Pass through a fine-mesh sieve/strainer to remove the tomato skins.

Add the cream and basil to the tomato soup and blitz again. Taste for seasoning and add more salt and pepper to taste.

Swirl a little pesto on top of the soup, or serve the pesto on the side for everyone to add their own. Serve straight away. This soup goes really well with a panini.

CLASSIC PEA SOUP

This vibrant green soup speckled with freshly ground black pepper is sweet, delicious and oh-so-simple to make. I like to serve it with American biscuits, sliced and filled with thickly carved ham – the perfect accompaniment for this classic soup.

1 onion, finely chopped
1 tablespoon olive oil
1 garlic clove, sliced
500 g/1 lb. 2 oz. frozen peas
1 litre/4 cups vegetable stock
125 ml/½ cup milk or cream
salt and pepper

TO SERVE (OPTIONAL)
1 x quantity Buttermilk Biscuits (see page 166)
50 g/3½ tablespoons soft butter
Worcestershire sauce, to taste
1 teaspoon wholegrain mustard
4 slices thick-cut ham

SERVES 4

Add the chopped onion to a saucepan with the olive oil and fry over a gentle heat until the onion is soft and translucent. Add the garlic and fry until it just starts to turn golden brown, taking care that it does not burn. Add a few drops of water to the saucepan if the onion and garlic start to brown too much.

Add the peas and stock to the saucepan and simmer for about 5 minutes until the peas are just soft. Add the milk or cream and blitz until very smooth in a blender or food processor, or use a stick blender. Return to the saucepan and season to taste with salt and pepper.

I serve this soup with filled buttermilk biscuits. To make mustard butter, whisk the soft butter, a dash of Worcestershire sauce and the mustard together. To serve, once you remove the biscuits from the oven, cut them in half, spread with the butter and place a slice of ham into each.

Serve the soup hot with an extra sprinkling of black pepper, and with the warm filled biscuits on the side. Tuck in straight away.

LEEK & POTATO SOUP

Leek and potato soup is one of the most comforting soups I know. Creamy and luxurious with a hint of mustard, here it is served with a crispy leek garnish on top. Add a simple cheese toastie/grilled cheese on the side for a more filling meal, if you like.

350 g/¾ lb. leeks, trimmed
50 g/3½ tablespoons butter
350 g/¾ lb. new potatoes or white potatoes
800 ml/generous 3¼ cups vegetable stock
2 teaspoons wholegrain mustard
salt and pepper
vegetable oil, for frying
cheese toasties, to serve (optional)

SERVES 4

Reserve about one-third of one of the leeks to make the fried leeks for the topping. Slice the remaining leeks and rinse them well. Place the leeks in a large saucepan with the butter and fry over a gentle heat until the leeks are soft.

If you are using white potatoes, peel them and cut them into chunks and add to the saucepan. If you are using new potatoes, simply halve them and place them in the saucepan with their skins on. Add the stock and mustard to the saucepan and simmer for about 25–30 minutes until the potatoes are soft. Season with salt and pepper.

Blend the soup in a blender or food processor until smooth, or use a stick blender. If you prefer a chunkier soup, blend half of the soup and leave half of it chunky to add texture.

For the leek garnish, finely slice the reserved leeks into very thin strips. Heat some vegetable oil in a small saucepan and fry the leeks until they are crispy. Remove from the oil and drain on paper towels. Sprinkle with a little salt to season.

Serve the soup in bowls or mugs, sprinkled with the crispy leeks. Serve with a cheese toastie/grilled cheese on the side, if you like.

SPICED LENTIL SOUP

This soup is inspired by my good friend Steven Wallis, winner of UK MasterChef in 2007 and an all-round amazing chef who cooks the best curries I know. It is a subtly spiced Indian dhal with coconut, finished with a tadka (spiced butter). It is perfect served with naan for dipping.

400 ml/scant 1¾ cups coconut milk
200 g/generous 1 cup red split lentils
1 large red chilli/chile
4 large vine tomatoes
2.5-cm/1-inch piece of ginger, peeled and finely chopped
1 teaspoon fenugreek
1 tablespoon garam masala
salt and pepper
2 large naan breads, sliced, to serve (optional)

FOR THE TADKA
2 tablespoons ghee or clarified butter
1 large garlic clove, finely sliced
6 curry leaves
1 tablespoon black onion/ nigella seeds

SERVES 4

For the soup, heat 800 ml/generous 3¼ cups water and the coconut milk in a large saucepan and pour in the lentils and a pinch of salt. Cut a slit in the chilli/chile but keep it whole as you will remove it later. Halve the tomatoes and add to the saucepan with the ginger, fenugreek and garam masala. Simmer for about 30 minutes until the lentils are soft. Remove the chilli/chile and discard it, or if you like a more spicy soup remove the stalk of the chile and return to the pot before blitzing. Transfer the soup to a blender or food processor and blitz until smooth, or use a stick blender. Return to the saucepan and season well with salt and pepper.

To prepare the tadka, heat the ghee in a small frying pan/skillet or pan then add the garlic, curry leaves and black onion/nigella seeds and fry until the garlic just starts to turn golden brown. Take care that it does not burn. Pour the soup, reheated if it has cooled, into four bowls and then top each with a spoonful of the tadka, which diners should stir into the soup. Serve straight away with slices of naan on the side, if you like.

FRENCH ONION SOUP

French onion soup is my go-to 'therapy' cooking. In order to maximize the flavour of this soup, it is really important to caramelize the onions until golden brown, so that they release a rich sweetness into the soup. As this requires you to stir continuously for some time, I suggest you pour yourself a large glass of wine and lose yourself in your thoughts as you do so!

600 g/1 lb. 5 oz. onions
50 g/3½ tablespoons butter
1 tablespoon olive oil
1 teaspoon white sugar
125 ml/½ cup sherry or brandy
800 ml/generous 3¼ cups beef stock
salt and pepper
Welsh rarebit toasties, to serve (optional)

a mandoline (optional)

SERVES 4

Slice the onions very finely either using a sharp knife or a mandoline. Place the onions in a heavy-based saucepan with the butter and olive oil. Season with a pinch of salt and sweat the onions down over a gentle heat for about 15 minutes until they become soft and translucent and start to caramelize. Take care that they do not burn as this will add bitterness to the soup. Add a good grind of black pepper to the saucepan with the sugar and stir for a few minutes more.

Add the sherry or brandy to the saucepan and simmer for a few minutes to cook off the alcohol. Add the stock to the saucepan and simmer for 5 minutes, then taste for seasoning, adding a little more salt and pepper if needed. If you prefer a smooth soup, you can blend it at this stage, although traditionally this soup is not blended.

To serve, pour the soup into four bowls and serve straight away. It is nice served with Welsh rarebit toasts (see page 11), if you want to make it a more substantial meal.

MINESTRONE

My partner's favourite soup is a minestrone 'cup a soup' (sad but true!) so I had a tall order to try and impress him with this recipe – luckily it worked, and this is now a firm family favourite. This is the perfect soup for using up leftover vegetables and there is no hard and fast rule on what to include. To make a vegetarian version, omit the pancetta, use vegetable stock rather than chicken stock and use a vegetarian Parmesan-style cheese.

2 tablespoons olive oil
1 onion, finely chopped
2 garlic cloves, peeled and finely chopped
70 g/2½ oz. cubed pancetta
1 courgette/zucchini, cut into small pieces
1 (bell) pepper, deseeded and cut into small pieces
1 large carrot, peeled and cut into small pieces
1 teaspoon dried oregano
a handful of fresh basil, chopped
a sprig of fresh rosemary
1 tablespoon tomato purée/paste
100 ml/⅓ cup plus 1 tablespoon white wine
400-g/14-oz. can chopped tomatoes
1 litre/4 cups chicken or vegetable stock
100 g/3½ oz. soup pasta

TO SERVE
fresh basil
croûtons (see page 10)
freshly grated Parmesan

SERVES 6

In a large saucepan, heat the olive oil with the onion and sauté until it is soft and translucent. Add the garlic and pancetta and fry for a few minutes until the pancetta is cooked and the garlic is lightly golden.

Add the courgette/zucchini, (bell) pepper and carrot and sauté for a few minutes with the oregano, basil and rosemary, then add the tomato purée/paste and white wine and cook for a few minutes.

Add the chopped tomatoes and stock and cook for 20–30 minutes until the vegetables are soft.

Add the soup pasta and cook for the time on the packet instructions, usually around 8–10 minutes. If the soup is too thick, add another 500 ml/2 cups of stock or water.

Check that the pasta is cooked before serving with freshly chopped basil, croûtons and plenty of freshly grated Parmesan.

CREAMY CAULIFLOWER & BLUE CHEESE SOUP

Cauliflower may seem a humble vegetable but in this recipe, it is transformed into a creamy soup packed with flavour. If you don't have cauliflower, you can substitute broccoli, which works equally well. If blue cheese is not your favourite, try Cheddar instead.

15 g/1 tablespoon butter
1 onion, finely chopped
1 whole cauliflower about 850 g/1 lb. 14 oz., leaves and stalk removed, chopped into pieces
1 litre/4 cups vegetable stock
125 ml/½ cup milk
75 g/2¾ oz. soft blue cheese, plus extra to serve (optional)
salt and pepper

SERVES 4

In a saucepan, melt the butter and fry the onion until soft and translucent. Add the cauliflower to the saucepan together with the stock and simmer until the cauliflower is very soft.

Add the milk to the saucepan and season well with salt and pepper. Add the blue cheese and stir over the heat until it has melted, then blend in a blender or food processor until very smooth and creamy, or use a stick blender. Season with salt and pepper to taste.

Pour into four bowls and top each with a sprinkling of black pepper and a little extra blue cheese, if liked.

ASPARAGUS SOUP WITH POACHED EGGS

For a little bit of luxury, asparagus is my first choice. I never really understood how exquisite it was until my friend Kathy Brown picked some in her garden and we cooked it in butter within 5 minutes of picking – the taste was sublime. It is best to use asparagus when it is in season, as out of season it generally has to travel a long way and loses its fresh crispness.

300 g/10½ oz. thin asparagus, ends trimmed
100 g/7 tablespoons butter
1 shallot, finely chopped
750 ml/3 cups chicken stock
250 ml/1 cup double/heavy cream or milk
1 teaspoon distilled white vinegar or white wine vinegar
4 very fresh eggs
salt and pepper
olive oil, to drizzle
toasted baguette slices, to serve

SERVES 4

Begin by removing the asparagus tips. To do this hold each asparagus spear in your hands and bend it so that it snaps at its natural point which will be a few centimetres/an inch or so below the tip.

Heat the butter in a saucepan until it starts to turn light golden and smells nutty. Take care not to burn it. Add the asparagus tips to the pan (reserve the stalks for later in the recipe) and cook for 3–5 minutes until just tender. Remove the asparagus, leaving the butter in the pan, and season well with salt and pepper. Set aside until you are ready to serve.

For the soup, return the saucepan with the brown butter to the heat and add the chopped shallot. Cook over a gentle heat until soft and translucent. Roughly chop the asparagus stalks, add to the pan and cook for a few minutes, then add the stock and simmer for 20 minutes.

Add the cream or milk to the pan and simmer until warm. Blend the soup in a blender or food processor, or use a stick blender, then pass through a fine-mesh sieve/strainer to ensure that the soup is very smooth. Season to taste.

When you are ready to serve, bring the soup back to a simmer to keep it warm whilst you prepare the eggs. Add water to a large frying pan/skillet and add the vinegar. It is important to use really fresh eggs. Break the eggs, one by one, onto a plate or saucer and, moving the saucer very carefully, tip away any of the excess egg white (you only want the egg white that is attached to the yolk for the best poaching results). Swirl the water in the pan and then pour an egg into the centre of the swirl; this will help the egg to form an oval shape. Repeat with the remaining eggs and cook each for about 3 minutes. Remember which order you placed the eggs in the pan so that you remove them in the correct order.

Pour the hot soup into shallow bowls and place an egg in the centre of each, making sure that they eggs are well drained of water. Top each bowl with some of the asparagus tips and a sprinkling of cracked black pepper and serve straight away so that the yolks are nice and runny when you break into the egg. Serve with toasted baguette slices.

CULLEN SKINK

This was one of my dad's favourite soups – he often talked about the best Cullen skink he ever ate in Cromarty in Moray Firth! I had high standards to live up to with my recipe, but it received his seal of approval!

30 g/2 tablespoons butter
1 small onion, finely chopped
1 leek, finely sliced
400 g/14 oz. white potatoes, peeled and cut into chunks
125 ml/½ cup white wine
750 ml/3 cups fish or vegetable stock
1 teaspoon wholegrain mustard
240 g/8½ oz. smoked haddock (either undyed or yellow), skinned and deboned
about 300 ml/1¼ cups milk
1 bay leaf
5 whole peppercorns
125 ml/½ cup double/heavy cream
fresh chives, chopped, to garnish

SERVES 4

Heat the butter in a large saucepan and sauté the onion and leek until they are soft. Add the potatoes to the saucepan. Add the white wine and simmer for a few minutes, then add the stock and mustard and simmer until the potatoes are soft.

Meanwhile, prepare the fish. Place the fish in a small saucepan which is just large enough to hold the fish and cover with milk so that it is just covered (this should be approximately 300 ml/1¼ cups milk but the exact quantity will depend on the size of your saucepan). Add the bay leaf and peppercorns to the milk and poach the fish for 6–8 minutes until it is cooked through.

Remove from the milk and place on one side. Strain the milk into the soup, removing the peppercorns and bay leaf. Take two ladlefuls of the soup, including some of the potato, and blend in a blender or food processor until smooth, then return to the saucepan. This will thicken the soup.

Flake the fish into the soup in large chunks, making sure that there are no bones. Stir in the double/heavy cream and heat for a minute or two.

Serve straight away, sprinkled with freshly chopped chives.

CURRIED PARSNIP SOUP

Curried parsnip soup is one of the most traditional flavours of soup and is always popular. The sweetness of the vegetable pairs perfectly with the spices. This soup is topped with a traditional tadka of ghee with fried spices and curry leaves. I like quite a mild flavour so I use korma curry powder, but you can use a spicier version if you prefer. You can even add a finely sliced red chilli/chile at the same time as the garlic for extra fire. Parsnip crisps also make a fun topping – you can either buy these or make them in the same way as the carrot crisps in the recipe on page 123.

2 tablespoons ghee
1 onion, chopped
2 garlic cloves, finely chopped
2.5-cm/1-inch piece of ginger, peeled and finely sliced
500 g/1 lb. 2 oz. parsnips, peeled and chopped
1 tablespoon curry powder
1 litre/4 cups vegetable stock
salt and pepper

FOR THE TADKA
2 tablespoons ghee
1 teaspoon cumin seeds
1 teaspoon nigella seeds
12 curry leaves

SERVES 4

Heat the ghee in a large saucepan and fry the onion over a gentle heat until soft and translucent. Add the garlic and ginger and fry for few minutes. Add the parsnips and curry powder and cook for a few minutes, then add the stock and simmer until the parsnips are soft, which should take about 20–30 minutes.

Blitz the soup in a blender or food processor until smooth, or use a stick blender, and then season with salt and pepper to taste.

Heat the ghee for the tadka and add the cumin seeds, nigella seeds and curry leaves. Heat for a few minutes until you can smell the spices and the seeds start to pop.

Pour the soups into four bowls and top each with a little of the hot tadka to serve.

CREAM OF CHICKEN SOUP

Cream of chicken soup is probably one of the most popular soups – it is proper hug-in-a-mug stuff and, although you can buy good store-bought versions, it is worth taking the time to make it yourself. You can use leftover cooked chicken in place of the fresh chicken if you prefer, adding it to the pan with the stock and reducing the cooking time to 15 minutes. You can also replace the chicken thighs with breasts, but I prefer the stronger flavour you get from thigh meat.

1 tablespoon olive oil
1 onion, finely sliced
500 g/1 lb. 2 oz. boneless, skinless chicken thighs
2 garlic cloves, sliced
250 ml/1 cup white wine
1 litre/4 cups chicken or vegetable stock
250 ml/1 cup milk or double/heavy cream
salt and pepper
chopped fresh tarragon, to garnish (optional)

SERVES 4–6

In a large saucepan, heat the oil and sauté the onion until soft and translucent.

Cut the chicken thighs in half and add to the saucepan. Sear the chicken thigh pieces so that they are lightly golden brown on all sides. If your saucepan is too small, you can cook the chicken in batches.

Add the garlic to the saucepan and cook for a few minutes more.

Add the wine to the saucepan and simmer for a few minutes to burn off the alcohol, then add the stock, season with salt and pepper, and simmer the soup for around 30 minutes. Add the milk or cream to the saucepan and remove from the heat.

Remove half of the chicken from the saucepan using a slotted spoon and cut into small pieces. Set aside.

Blend the remaining soup in a blender or food processor until smooth, or use a stick blender, then return to the pan and add back in the cooked chopped chicken. Heat the soup and taste for seasoning, adding more salt and pepper if needed. Serve piping hot with a sprinkling of black pepper and some freshly chopped tarragon, if you like.

CHAPTER 2
SATISFYING SOUPS

PEARL BARLEY BROTH

There isn't a heartier farmhouse soup than pearl barley broth. The barley makes this a really filling soup, but if you don't have any, you can substitute with soup pasta instead. This version is made with lamb, but you can easily replace the lamb and lamb stock with beef and beef stock, if you prefer.

100 g/generous ½ cup pearl barley
1 tablespoon olive oil
1 onion, finely chopped
2 lamb leg steaks (about 300 g/10½ oz.)
3 carrots, peeled and cut into small cubes
100 ml/⅓ cup plus 1 tablespoon white wine
1 litre/4 cups lamb stock
1 heaped teaspoon wholegrain mustard
100 g/½ cup frozen peas
salt and pepper
chopped fresh parsley, to garnish (optional)

SERVES 4

Rinse the pearl barley. Drain and set aside.

Add the oil and onion to a large saucepan and sauté for about 5 minutes over a medium heat until the onion softens and starts to caramelize.

Cut the lamb steaks into small pieces, trimming away any fat, and add to the saucepan to brown. Once the lamb has browned on all sides, add the carrot pieces and pearl barley to the saucepan and sauté for a few minutes.

Pour in the wine and bring to a simmer, then pour in the lamb stock and 500 ml/2 cups of water. Gently simmer the soup for 30 minutes until the pearl barley is soft.

Using a blender or food processor, blend a few ladlefuls of the broth (including some barley and carrots) and return it to the soup to thicken it. Add the mustard and season with salt and pepper to taste.

When you are ready to serve, heat the soup, add in the frozen peas and cook for about 5 minutes. Pour into four bowls and serve sprinkled with freshly chopped parsley.

THREE BEAN SOUP

Beans are a great source of protein, especially for anyone on a vegan or vegetarian diet. You can use any beans of your choice for this soup. Canned beans are easy to use because they are already cooked, but you can prepare your own beans, if you prefer, by soaking them overnight and then cooking according to the packet instructions. The chilli/chili sauce with the kidney beans is generally very mild, so if you prefer a spicier heat, add a little chilli/chili powder or some dried chilli flakes/hot red pepper flakes when you add the beans for a fiery kick.

1 tablespoon olive oil
1 onion, chopped
1 garlic clove, finely chopped
1 yellow (bell) pepper, deseeded and cut into small pieces
1 carrot, peeled and cut into small pieces
1 courgette/zucchini, cut into small pieces
400-g/14-oz. can black beans in water, drained
400-g/14-oz. can cannellini beans in water, drained
400-g/14-oz. can red kidney beans in chilli/chili sauce
400-g/14-oz. can chopped tomatoes
1 tablespoon tomato purée/paste
250 ml/1 cup red wine
1 litre/4 cups chicken or vegetable stock
1 teaspoon dried oregano
a handful of chopped fresh basil, plus extra to serve
100 g/3½ oz. soup pasta
salt and pepper
freshly grated Parmesan or Cheddar, to serve

SERVES 6

In a large saucepan, heat the olive oil and fry the onion until soft and translucent. Add the chopped garlic and fry until lightly golden brown, then add the chopped (bell) pepper, carrot and courgette/zucchini and fry for a few minutes to soften.

Rinse the drained black beans and cannellini beans well in cold water. Add them to the saucepan along with the kidney beans in chilli/chili sauce, chopped tomatoes, tomato purée/paste, red wine, stock, oregano and basil and simmer for 30 minutes.

Add the soup pasta to the saucepan and simmer for the time stated on the pasta instructions – usually about 8–10 minutes – until the pasta is cooked. Season well with salt and pepper.

Using a stick blender, blender or food processor, blitz the soup quickly – you want to leave most of the soup in chunks, but blending some of the mixture will help thicken the soup. Taste for seasoning adding more salt and pepper as needed.

Divide the soup between six bowls and serve with freshly grated Parmesan or Cheddar and some extra chopped basil leaves.

ITALIAN WEDDING SOUP

In many parts of the world, it is traditional to serve soup as a first course at a wedding. This recipe is based on the traditional Italian wedding soup made with meatballs and simmered in broth with spinach and carrots. Italian sausagemeat/bulk sausage often contains fennel seeds and they give a wonderful aromatic flavour to this soup. Don't worry, you don't have to be celebrating a wedding to enjoy this soup – it makes a great supper or hearty lunch dish for any occasion. Traditionally the soup has small pasta in as well which you can add if you like, although I find it is filling enough without. If you do add pasta, add with the spinach and meatballs and simmer for the time on the packet instructions – usually about 10 minutes.

1 tablespoon olive oil
1 onion, finely chopped
1 garlic clove, finely chopped
65 g/2¼ oz. pancetta cubes
2 carrots, peeled and cut into small cubes
a small handful of fresh basil
a sprig of fresh rosemary
200 ml/¾ cup red wine
1.5 litres/6½ cups chicken stock
80 g/2¾ oz. spinach leaves

FOR THE MEATBALLS
1 teaspoon fennel seeds
200 g/7 oz. lean minced/ground beef
200 g/7 oz. lean minced/ground pork
1 small egg, beaten
30 g/scant 1 cup dried breadcrumbs, such as panko
45 g/⅔ cup finely grated Parmesan, plus extra to serve
salt and pepper

pestle and mortar
roasting pan, lined with baking parchment

SERVES 6

Begin by making the meatballs. Grind the fennel seeds in a pestle and mortar to a fine powder. In a bowl mix together the beef and pork, the ground fennel seeds, beaten egg, breadcrumbs and grated Parmesan. It is best to mix with clean hands so that everything is well mixed, or you can mix with a fork if you prefer. Season with salt and pepper. Shape into small balls about the size of a heaped teaspoon and small enough to be eaten in one mouthful. Place in the lined roasting pan and chill in the fridge for 30 minutes.

Meanwhile, preheat the oven to 180°C (350°F) Gas 4.

Bake the meatballs in the preheated oven for 10–15 minutes until golden brown, turning halfway through to ensure even cooking. Cut one in half to check that they are cooked through. Remove from the oven and place on paper towels to remove any excess fat. Cool, then store in the fridge until you are ready to serve your soup.

For the soup, place the olive oil in a large saucepan over a medium heat. Add the chopped onion and sauté until the onion is soft and starting to caramelize. Add the garlic and pancetta pieces and fry for a further 3–5 minutes until the pancetta is cooked through and the garlic is lightly golden brown. Add the carrots to the saucepan with the chopped basil, sprig of rosemary and the wine and simmer for a few minutes, then add the stock and simmer over a low heat for a further 20 minutes or so until the carrots are soft.

Season with salt and pepper. Shortly before you are ready to serve, add the meatballs and spinach to the saucepan and simmer for 10 minutes until the spinach is wilted and the meatballs are hot.

Serve with grated Parmesan and extra salt and pepper to taste.

THANKSGIVING TURKEY SOUP

Thanksgiving is celebrated with one of the most delicious meals of the year. I have been lucky enough to celebrate it with the wonderful Globus family in New York and never cease to be amazed at the table spread with the most enormous turkey, three different types of sweet potato and the obligatory can of cranberry jelly. This soup is inspired by that wonderful meal with tender turkey in a creamy soup speckled with cranberry jewels. It is perfect to make with leftover turkey as well as fresh turkey. To do this simply follow the alternative method in the recipe below.

1 tablespoon olive oil
1 white onion, finely chopped
2 turkey breasts (about 350 g/12 oz.), cut in half
1 large garlic clove, finely chopped
250 ml/1 cup white wine
1 litre/4 cups chicken stock
2 potatoes (approx. 200 g/7 oz.), peeled and cut into quarters
50 g/½ cup dried cranberries, plus extra to serve
Parmesan Popovers (see page 173), to serve

SERVES 4

In a large saucepan, heat the olive oil over a medium heat, add the onion and sauté until translucent and lightly golden brown. Add the turkey pieces and garlic and fry until the turkey is browned on all sides and the garlic is lightly golden brown. If the onion and garlic start to brown too much, add a spoonful of water to the saucepan.

Pour the wine into the saucepan and simmer for a few minutes and then add the chicken stock and potato. Simmer over a low heat for about 30 minutes until the potato is soft and the turkey is cooked.

Remove half of the turkey from the saucepan and blitz the remaining soup in a blender or food processor until smooth, or use a stick blender. Return the soup to the saucepan and add the cranberries, then bring back to a simmer. Cut the reserved cooked turkey into small pieces and return to the pan. Simmer for a few minutes. Serve hot, topped with extra dried cranberries.

If you are using leftover turkey, add half of this at the same time as the potatoes. Once you have blended the soup, add the remaining cooked turkey with the cranberries and simmer for 10 minutes until hot.

SAUSAGE & CABBAGE SOUP

This hearty soup reminds me of a trip to Germany with my friend Maren where we enjoyed a 'kohl und pinkelfahrt' – a long snowy trek through the woods, drinking schnapps, followed by steaming bowls of cabbage and sausage at the end of the walk. This soup has a meaty broth with sweetness from the cider and a tang of mustard seeds. If you prefer not to make the sausage balls, you can use cooked whole sausages instead and just cut them into slices and add to the soup. Make sure they are heated through in the soup broth before serving. To avoid having to slurp too much with this soup, make sure you cut the cabbage into short, finely shredded pieces.

3 pork sausages
1 tablespoon olive oil
1 large onion, finely chopped
125 g/4½ oz. bacon lardons
1 garlic clove, finely chopped
a large sprig of fresh rosemary
1 heaped teaspoon wholegrain mustard
300 ml/1¼ cups pear or apple cider
700 ml/scant 3 cups beef stock
1 small Savoy cabbage, stalk and outer leaves removed, finely shredded and rinsed

roasting pan, lined with baking parchment

SERVES 4

Preheat the oven to 180°C (350°F) Gas 4.

Remove the skins from sausages and roll the meat into small balls, about 6 or 7 from each sausage. You need them to be small enough to eat in a mouthful of soup. Place them in the lined roasting pan and bake in the oven for about 10 minutes until they are lightly golden brown, turning regularly so that they are golden brown all over. Drain on paper towels to remove any excess fat. Set aside whilst you prepare the soup.

In a large saucepan, heat the oil over a medium heat and fry the onions until soft and translucent. Add the lardons, garlic and rosemary to the saucepan and fry for a few minutes until the bacon is cooked through. Add the mustard to the saucepan and fry for 1 minute, then add the cider and stock and bring to a simmer, then cook over a low heat for 15 minutes. Add the finely shredded cabbage to the saucepan and continue to simmer for about 10 minutes until the cabbage is soft. Add the reserved sausage balls to the pan and heat for a further 5 minutes.

Season with salt and pepper, tasting before adding too much salt as the soup will already contain some salt from the bacon. Remove the rosemary sprig before serving into bowls, making sure that the sausage balls are evenly distributed.

BRUSSELS SPROUT & CHESTNUT SOUP

Brussels sprouts are one of those love-them-or-hate-them vegetables – much misunderstood! When roasted, they take on a lovely, caramelized flavour and make a wonderful warming soup. With deep, rich flavours of bacon and chestnut mixed with the sprouts, even a die-hard sprout hater may be converted with this recipe!

500 g/1 lb. 2 oz. Brussels sprouts
125 g/4½ oz. bacon lardons
100 g/7 tablespoons butter
180 g/6½ oz. whole peeled chestnuts
1 tablespoon olive oil
250 ml/1 cup white wine
1 litre/4 cups chicken or vegetable stock
4 tablespoons crème fraîche or sour cream
salt and black pepper

SERVES 4

Preheat the oven to 200°C (400°F) Gas 6.

Trim the ends from the Brussels sprouts, removing any outer leaves which are blemished. Cut any large sprouts in half. Place them in a deep roasting pan with the lardons, butter and chestnuts and season well with pepper. There is no need to add salt at this stage as the salt from the bacon will season the soup. Bake in the preheated oven for about 30 minutes until the sprouts start to char slightly.

Remove a large spoonful of the sprouts, bacon and chestnut mixture for the garnish. Remove and discard any burnt leaves from the sprouts, as these will make the soup taste bitter.

Reduce the oven temperature to 180°C (350°F) Gas 4. Add the wine and stock to the roasting pan and bake for a further 20 minutes.

Blend the contents of the pan in a blender or food processor until the soup is smooth, or use a stick blender.

Taste for seasoning and add some salt and more pepper as needed. Pour the soup into four bowls, add a spoonful of crème fraîche or sour cream to each bowl and swirl it in.

Chop the reserved Brussels sprouts, chestnuts and bacon into small pieces and serve on top of the hot soup with an extra sprinkling of black pepper.

ROASTED GARLIC SOUP

As everyone knows, garlic can have quite a pungent taste, but when it is roasted it softens and caramelizes and takes on a wonderful earthy flavour of forest walks and mushrooms. If you want, you can add mushrooms as well to give the soup more body. Don't be scared about using four whole bulbs of garlic here!

30 g/2 tablespoons butter
2 large onions, finely chopped
60 ml/4 tablespoons brandy
1 litre/4 cups beef stock
freshly squeezed juice of ½ lemon

FOR THE ROASTED GARLIC
a large sprig of fresh rosemary
a few sprigs of fresh thyme
strips of zest from 1 lemon
4 whole garlic bulbs
olive oil, to drizzle
salt and pepper

SERVES 4

Preheat the oven to 180°C (350°F) Gas 4.

Start by making the roasted garlic. Place the rosemary, thyme and lemon zest strips in a roasting pan and put the four whole garlic bulbs on top of the herbs. Drizzle the bulbs with a good drizzle of olive oil and season with salt and pepper. Roast in the preheated oven for 25–30 minutes until the bulbs feel soft inside when you press them. Leave to cool.

Once the garlic bulbs are cool, cut them in half with a sharp knife and squeeze out the garlic, which will be creamy and paste like. Discard all of the garlic skins, making sure that no skin is left in the garlic paste. Reserve some of the roasted thyme to garnish the soup and discard the other herbs and the zest but mix any oil with the garlic paste to add flavour.

For the soup, heat the butter in a saucepan over medium heat and fry the onions in the butter until soft and translucent and starting to caramelize. Add the garlic purée and cook for a few minutes more. Add the brandy and cook until it is almost evaporated, then add the stock and lemon juice, bring it to a simmer and then cook over a low heat for about 10 minutes.

Blitz the soup in a blender or food processor until smooth, or use a stick blender. Taste and adjust the seasoning, and then serve in bowls with the reserved sprigs of roasted thyme to garnish.

If you prefer a thicker texture soup you can add 2 peeled and cubed potatoes with the stock and simmer until the potatoes are soft.

PRAWN/SHRIMP GUMBO SOUP

Gumbo originated in Louisiana and is filled with the tastes of the South with Creole spices and the traditional 'holy trinity' of (bell) peppers, onions and celery. Traditionally, gumbo is a stew, thickened with okra, but as this is a soup, I have omitted the okra and just thickened the soup with the traditional golden roux that gives gumbo its classic flavour. This soup is made with prawns/shrimp and chorizo and has a wonderful richness that everyone is sure to enjoy.

1 tablespoon olive oil
1 onion, finely sliced
2 (bell) peppers, deseeded and finely chopped
2 sticks/ribs celery, finely sliced
125 g/4½ oz. cooking chorizo, cut into slices
2 teaspoons Cajun spice mix
750 ml/3 cups chicken stock
500 g/2 cups passata/strained tomatoes
30 ml/2 tablespoons sherry or brandy
225 g/8 oz. raw king prawns/jumbo shrimp, peeled and deveined
cornbread, to serve (try Cheesy Chilli/Chile Cornbread on page 169 or Cornbread Muffins on page 167)

FOR THE ROUX
90 g/6 tablespoons butter
70 g/½ cup plain/all-purpose flour
salt and pepper

SERVES 4–6

In a large saucepan, heat the oil over a medium heat and fry the onion, (bell) peppers and celery until very soft. Add the chorizo slices and fry until they start to caramelize. Add the spice mix and fry for 1–2 minutes, then add the stock, passata/strained tomatoes and sherry. Simmer for about 30–40 minutes and season with salt and pepper.

For the roux, melt the butter in a saucepan and add the flour. Whisk constantly over a gentle heat. It is important to keep whisking so that it does not burn. The roux will start to turn golden brown and will smell nutty. This will take around 5 minutes or so, so be patient. When it is a deep golden brown, add it to the soup, whisking all the time and the soup will thicken quickly.

Cut a slit down the back of each prawn/shrimp and then add them to the hot soup. Simmer until the prawns/shrimp are pink and cooked through, which will take about 5 minutes. Taste for seasoning adding salt and pepper to your taste.

Divide into bowls and serve hot with cornbread on the side.

SMOKY BLACK BEAN SOUP

On a trip to Costa Rica I stayed at the most wonderful organic finca just outside San José called Finca Rosa Blanca. The food was all sourced locally and one of the highlights was their black bean soup. Serve it with warm cornbread muffins on the side, if you like.

1 tablespoon olive oil
1 onion, finely chopped
2.5-cm/1-inch piece of ginger, peeled and finely chopped
1 garlic clove, finely chopped
1 large red chilli/chile, deseeded and finely chopped
15 g/1 tablespoon butter
6 tomatoes
1 teaspoon smoked paprika
½ teaspoon cayenne pepper
1 teaspoon ground cumin
1 teaspoon ground cinnamon
½ teaspoon ground allspice
2 x 400-g/14-oz. cans black beans, drained
800 ml/3¼ cups vegetable or chicken stock
a handful of chopped fresh coriander/cilantro
1 avocado, pitted and peeled
freshly squeezed juice of 1 lime
4 tablespoons sour cream
salt and pepper
Cornbread Muffins (see page 167), to serve

SERVES 4

In a large saucepan, heat the oil and sauté the onion until soft and translucent. Add the ginger and garlic and sauté until the garlic is lightly golden brown. Reserve a few pieces of chilli/chile for the garnish and add the remainder to the pan with the butter. Cook until the chilli/chile starts to soften.

Blitz the tomatoes in a blender or food processor to a smooth purée. Set aside.

Add the paprika, cayenne pepper, cumin, cinnamon and allspice to the saucepan and fry in the oil for a minute to release the flavours.

Rinse the drained black beans and add to the saucepan with the stock and puréed tomatoes. Simmer for about 20–30 minutes, then season with salt and pepper to taste and stir in the chopped coriander/cilantro.

Chop the avocado into small pieces and toss in the lime juice to prevent it discolouring.

Pour the warm soup into four bowls and top each with a spoonful of sour cream, some avocado pieces and the reserved chilli/chile pieces.

Serve with cornbread muffins on the side.

KOREAN BEEF BROTH

This tasty broth has very few ingredients. It simply requires patience while the beef brisket simmers in the stock for a couple of hours.

500 g/1 lb. 2 oz. beef brisket
1 onion, chopped
3 spring onions/scallions, sliced
2.5-cm/1-inch piece of ginger, peeled and sliced
1 beef stock pot or cube
salt and pepper
a few fresh coriander/cilantro leaves, to garnish

SERVES 4

Heat a griddle pan/ridged grill pan until very hot and then sear the beef on all sides. Place the seared beef in a large saucepan with 2 litres/8 cups of water. Add the onion, spring onions/scallions, ginger and stock cube. Bring to the boil, then reduce the heat and simmer for about 2 hours until the liquid has reduced significantly, skimming any fat and impurities from the surface.

Remove the beef and strain the broth through a fine-mesh sieve/strainer – discard the vegetables and retain the liquid. Season with salt and pepper. Allow the liquid to cool and then chill in the refrigerator. Store the beef in the refrigerator as well.

When the soup has chilled and you are ready to eat, remove any fat which has set on the surface of the soup and then reheat in a saucepan. Cut the beef into very thin slices and place some in the centre of each soup bowl. Use any remaining beef to make some beef and kimchi toasties to serve on the side, if you like.

Pour the warm broth into the bowls and garnish with some coriander/ cilantro leaves.

KIMCHI GRILLED CHEESE

Kimchi pickle is a national dish of Korea and in this recipe it is used as a delicious cheese toastie filling along with slices of beef.

30 g/2 tablespoons soft butter
8 slices bread
thin slices brisket (from the soup recipe above)
12 slices cheese (such as cheddar or Monterey jack)
4 tablespoons kimchi pickle

SERVES 4

While the soup is reheating, butter one side of each slice of bread. On one non-buttered side, place slices of the beef, three slices of cheese and top with a tablespoon of kimchi pickle. Cover with a second slice of bread, butter-side up, and then fry in a griddle pan for about 3 minutes on each side until the cheese has melted and the sandwich is golden brown. Repeat with the remaining sandwiches. Depending on the size of your pan you will probably need to cook the sandwiches in batches.

Serve as a side to the Korean broth.

CHAPTER 3

SOUPS FOR THE SOUL

CHINESE HOT & SOUR SOUP

This hot and sour soup has an amazing flavour and texture. I love enoki mushrooms – they look like something from a fairytale – but if you can't find them, you can substitute button/white mushrooms instead.

1 litre/4 cups chicken stock
140 g/5 oz. water chestnuts
2.5-cm/1-inch piece ginger, peeled and finely chopped
2 large oyster mushrooms
20 enoki mushrooms
1 garlic clove, finely chopped
2 tablespoons dark soy sauce
1 tablespoon fish sauce
1 red chilli/chile, deseeded and finely sliced
1 tablespoon tomato purée/paste
200 g/7 oz. cooked chicken
100 g/1 cup sugar snap peas, sliced
100 g/¾ cup frozen peas
3 spring onions/scallions, finely sliced
1 egg, beaten
2 tablespoons sherry vinegar
2 tablespoons cornflour/cornstarch
summer rolls, to serve (optional)

SERVES 4

Pour the stock into a saucepan and heat over a gentle heat. Slice the water chestnuts and add to the stock along with the ginger, mushrooms, garlic, soy sauce, fish sauce, sliced chilli/chile and tomato purée/paste. Simmer for about 5 minutes until the mushrooms are soft.

Coarsely chop the chicken and add it to the saucepan along with the sugar snap peas, frozen peas and spring onions/scallions. Simmer for a further 5 minutes to allow the peas to cook.

Very slowly pour the beaten egg into the soup in a thin line so that it cooks in small pieces in the soup. Mix the vinegar with the cornflour/cornstarch to make a smooth paste. Take a ladleful of the stock from the soup (without any of the solid ingredients), add the cornflour/cornstarch mixture and whisk well to dissolve. It is important to do this – if you just add the paste to the soup, you can end up with lumps of cornflour/cornstarch jelly which ruin the soup. Add the ladleful of soup back into the saucepan and whisk it over the heat to thicken it.

Ladle into four bowls and serve with some summer rolls on the side, if you like.

VIETNAMESE VEGETABLE PHO

Vietnamese cooking is fresh and fragrant with the perfect combination of sweet, salty and savoury. Pho is a simple broth in which you poach vegetables, adding seasonings of your choosing. If you can find Thai basil, use it for an authentic taste. Omit the fish sauce for veggies.

1 tablespoon olive oil
1 onion, finely sliced
1 garlic clove, finely sliced
2.5-cm/1-inch piece ginger, peeled and finely sliced
2 star anise
1 teaspoon ground cinnamon
½ teaspoon dried chilli flakes/ hot red pepper flakes
1 tablespoon chopped fresh coriander/cilantro
1 tablespoon chopped fresh basil (Thai basil if available)
1 tablespoon soy sauce
1 tablespoon fish sauce
1 litre/quart vegetable stock
1 carrot, peeled
1 pak choi/bok choy
2 spring onions/scallions, finely sliced
150 g/5½ oz. mushrooms, sliced
freshly squeezed juice of 2 limes
2 teaspoons white sugar
80 g/3 oz. ramen noodles
bahn mi, to serve (optional)

SERVES 4

In a large saucepan, heat the oil and fry the onion, garlic and ginger slices until the onion is soft. Add the star anise, cinnamon and dried chilli flakes/hot red pepper flakes to the saucepan and fry for a further minute. Add the coriander/cilantro, basil, soy sauce, fish sauce and stock and simmer for about 10 minutes.

Finely slice the carrot into ribbons using a swivel peeler and add to the saucepan. Trim the pak choi/bok choy and slice lengthways. Add the carrot, pak choi/bok choy, spring onions/scallions and mushrooms to the saucepan. Pour in the lime juice, add the sugar and simmer for 5 minutes.

Add the noodles and cook for a further 5 minutes. Remove the star anise and then pour the soup into four bowls to serve. Serve with Vietnamese-style bahn mi smoked tofu and vegetable filled baguette for a heartier meal, if you like.

HORSERADISH BORSCHT

Beetroot/beets make one of the most amazing coloured soups I know. This one is delicately flavoured with orange and apple and a kick of horseradish. Serve it with dark rye bread topped with a cream cheese and chives, if you want to add a bit of contrast to this earthy soup.

450 g/1 lb. fresh beetroot/beets
2 onions
1–2 tablespoons olive oil
100 g/3½ oz. new potatoes or white potatoes
1 cooking apple
freshly squeezed juice of 2 oranges
1 tablespoon creamed horseradish sauce
800 ml/generous 3¼ cups beef or vegetable stock
4 tablespoons cream (optional)
salt and pepper
rye toasts, topped with cream cheese and chives, to serve (optional)

SERVES 4

Preheat the oven to 180°C (350°F) Gas 4.

Begin by peeling the beetroot/beets and onions, then chop both the onions and beetroot/beets into wedges and place in a roasting pan. Drizzle with a little olive oil and season with salt and pepper. Roast in the preheated oven for about 30 minutes until the beetroot/beets are just soft. If the onions start to brown before the beetroot/beets are cooked, remove them from the oven and set aside until the beetroot/beets are ready. You can tell they are cooked when a sharp knife slides out easily.

Place the roasted beetroot/beets and onions in a large saucepan. If you are using new potatoes, cut them in half and place in the saucepan without removing the skins. If you are using larger white potatoes, peel them and cut into pieces, then place in the saucepan. Peel and core the apple, chop it into pieces and add to the saucepan. Add the orange juice, horseradish and stock to the saucepan, bring to the boil, then reduce the heat and simmer for about 20–30 minutes until the potatoes are soft.

Pour the soup into a blender or food processor and blitz until smooth, or use a stick blender. Return to the saucepan and warm through again, then pour the soup into four bowls. Swirl a drizzle of cream over the top of each portion, if using. Serve with rye toasts topped with cream cheese and chives, if you like.

CHILLED AVOCADO SOUP WITH CRAB SALAD

On summer days there is nothing nicer to serve for an appetizer or light lunch in the sunshine that a chilled summer soup. This soup has a thick and creamy consistency, but you can add more stock if you want a thinner soup. The soup is rich, so you only need to serve small bowlfuls (or glassfuls), and is topped with a fresh and spicy crab salad. It looks very pretty served in little glasses or fine bone china teacups.

4 ripe avocados, pitted and peeled
freshly squeezed juice of 3 limes
400 ml/1¾ cups vegetable stock, chilled
200 ml/¾ cup single/light cream
2 tablespoons chopped fresh coriander/cilantro, plus extra to garnish
salt and pepper
lime wedges, to serve

FOR THE CRAB SALAD
60 g/2 oz. white crab meat
1 red chilli/chile, finely chopped
1 tablespoon olive oil
1 tablespoon chopped fresh coriander/cilantro

SERVES 4

Take half of an avocado, chop into small pieces and drizzle with the juice of one lime. Set aside to add to the crab salad at the end.

Put the remaining avocados in a blender or food processor with the juice of the remaining two limes, the stock, cream and the coriander/cilantro and blend to a smooth purée. Season with salt and pepper.

For the crab salad, mix the crab with the reserved chopped avocado in lime juice, the chilli/chile and olive oil and season with salt and pepper.

Divide the soup between four glasses, cups or small bowls and place a spoonful of the salad on top of each portion. Serve straight away with lime wedges on the side.

ROASTED CAULIFLOWER SOUP
WITH TOASTED ALMONDS & PICKLED FLORETS

When cauliflower is roasted it takes on a whole new dimension with a caramelized flavour. Almonds add a rich nutty texture and the puréed cauliflower gives it a creamy feel even though there is no cream or milk added to the soup. This recipe is served with cauliflower pickles, which have a sharpness to cut through the creamy texture of the soup. The pickles should be prepared the day before so that they have time to absorb the wonderful vibrant yellow of the saffron.

a head of cauliflower, about 1 kg/2 lb. 4 oz.
olive oil, to drizzle
1 teaspoon sweet paprika, plus extra to dust
100 g/¾ cup blanched whole almonds (such as marcona)
1 litre/4 cups vegetable or chicken stock
4–6 tablespoons crème fraîche (optional)
salt and pepper

FOR THE PICKLED FLORETS
a pinch of saffron
2 tablespoons cider vinegar
1 tablespoon caster/granulated sugar

SERVES 4–6

Begin by making the pickled florets as these are best made the day before. Remove all the leaves from the cauliflower and remove one large floret from the base. Keep the rest of the cauliflower for making the soup. Slice the floret very finely and place in a bowl. Put the saffron into another small bowl, pour a little boiling water over and leave for 5 minutes to steep, then pour into the bowl with the cauliflower slices. Mix the sugar and vinegar together until the sugar has dissolved, and then add to the cauliflower and saffron water. Cover and place in the fridge to soak overnight.

The next day, preheat the oven to 200°C (400°F) Gas 6.

Using a sharp knife, remove the stalk of the cauliflower, but cut carefully to ensure that the head of the cauliflower stays in one piece. Place in the roasting pan, drizzle with a good glug of olive oil and sprinkle with salt, pepper and the paprika. Seal the pan with a layer of aluminium foil. Roast in the preheated oven for 45 minutes, then remove the foil and roast for a further 30–45 minutes until the cauliflower is soft.

About 5 minutes before the end of cooking, add the almonds to the roasting pan and roast for 5 minutes, which should colour the nuts a golden brown. Take care that they do not burn. Remove a handful of the nuts for the garnish and roughly chop them.

Place the cauliflower head (which will by now be really soft) in a large saucepan with the remaining nuts and add the stock. Bring to the boil over a medium heat, then reduce the heat and simmer for 10 minutes. Blend in a blender or food processor until smooth, or use a stick blender.

Pour into bowls and add a spoonful of crème fraîche, if using, to each portion. Sprinkle with the reserved chopped nuts and the pickled florets, and dust with a little paprika to finish.

SPINACH & NUTMEG SOUP

Spinach and nutmeg are a delicious combination – I love the heady smell of nutmeg and it really does transform this dish. Spinach is full of vitamins and is one of those super greens that are good for you in so many ways. This is such a quick soup to prepare and a great after-work supper.

2 tablespoons butter or olive oil
1 onion, finely chopped
160 g/5½ oz. spinach
1 litre/4 cups chicken or vegetable stock
250 g/9 oz. white potatoes, peeled and cut into small cubes
a pinch of grated nutmeg
100 ml/⅓ cup plus 1 tablespoon double/heavy cream
salt and pepper
Pangrattato (see page 10) or Garlic Croûtons (see page 10), to serve

SERVES 4

Heat the butter or oil in a large saucepan over medium heat and sauté the chopped onion until soft and translucent. Add the spinach, stock and potatoes to the saucepan and simmer for about 15–20 minutes until the potatoes are soft.

Season with salt and pepper and a good pinch of freshly grated nutmeg. Blitz in a blender or food processor until the soup is smooth, or use a stick blender. Pour back into the saucepan and add the double/heavy cream to the soup, then heat through gently.

Serve straight away with pangrattato or croûtons.

BROWN BUTTER BAKED POTATO SOUP

There are few things more comforting than a baked potato – and this soup takes all the flavours of a jacket with the addition of caramelized butter for a bit of luxury. Rich and creamy with sour cream and grated cheese, this is a perfect soup for cold winter days.

4 large baking potatoes
110 g/7¾ tablespoons butter
1 litre/4 cups chicken or vegetable stock
150 ml/⅔ cup sour cream
100 g/1 cup plus 2 tablespoons grated Cheddar
olive oil, to drizzle
salt and pepper

FOR THE SKINS
potato skins, reserved from the baked potatoes
olive oil, to drizzle
30 g/⅓ cup grated Cheddar

SERVES 4

Preheat the oven to 200°C (400°F) Gas 6.

Prick the potatoes with a fork, rub the skins with a little salt and bake in the preheated oven for about 1 hour until the potatoes are soft when you insert a sharp knife into the centre. Set aside until cool enough to handle without burning yourself.

In a saucepan, melt the butter over a gentle heat until it starts to lightly brown – the butter will smell nutty which is how you will know it is ready. Scoop out the potato from the skins (reserving the skins for the garnish) and add to the butter. Cook for a few minutes, then add the stock and simmer for 5–10 minutes. Add the sour cream and grated cheese, then blitz the soup in a blender or food processor until smooth, or use a stick blender. Pour the soup back into the saucepan, season with salt and pepper to taste and keep warm.

For the potato skins, preheat the grill/broiler to high. Place the reserved skins on a baking sheet and drizzle with a little olive oil. Sprinkle with the grated cheese and season with salt and pepper. Place under the hot grill/broiler and grill/broil until the cheese has melted and the skins are crispy – this will take about 5 minutes, but watch them carefully as grills/broilers are all different and you don't want them to burn.

Serve the soup in bowls with a drizzle of olive oil and the crispy potato skins broken up on top or served whole on the side.

SUNSHINE SOUP

This is a happy soup – the colour is vibrant yellow and, sprinkled with dried petals, it makes a perfect summer dish. The soup is also light and healthy and, in my view, good for the soul. If you want to make the soup thicker, add two peeled and chopped potatoes when you add the stock, simmer until the potatoes are soft, and then blend. Use vegetable stock to make the soup suitable for vegetarians.

2 whole corn cobs/ears
2 tablespoons olive oil
1 onion, chopped
3 yellow (bell) peppers, deseeded and cut into chunks
1 litre/4 cups chicken or vegetable stock
freshly squeezed juice of 1 lemon
marigold and cornflower petals, to garnish
Pangrattato (see page 10), to serve (optional)

SERVES 4

Using a sharp knife, on a chopping board, slice the kernels from the corn cobs/ears. Add these to a saucepan with the olive oil and onion and cook over a low heat until the onion is soft and translucent. Add the (bell) peppers and cook until they are soft. Add the stock and lemon juice and simmer for 15–20 minutes.

Blitz with a blender or food processor, or use a stick blender, then pass through a fine-mesh sieve/strainer or moulin to remove the corn and (bell) pepper skins and to make the soup smooth. Put the soup back in the saucepan and heat through again.

Pour the soup into four bowls and garnish with dried marigold and cornflower petals. Serve with pangrattato, if you like.

SWEET POTATO, CORIANDER/CILANTRO & MAPLE SOUP

Sweet potato is a perfect vegetable for soup as it has a smooth, silky and creamy texture. This is one of my favourite soups, packed with sweet and salty flavours. If you are serving to anyone who cannot eat gluten, make sure that the soy sauce you use is gluten-free, as not all brands are. This is a 'simmer' soup and needs no cooking steps other than putting everything in a pot to simmer – it's as easy as that!

1 litre/4 cups chicken stock
500 g/1 lb. 2 oz. sweet potatoes, peeled and chopped
50 g/2 oz. fresh coriander/cilantro, plus extra to garnish
40 ml/2½ tablespoons pure maple syrup
40 ml/2½ tablespoons soy sauce
freshly squeezed juice of 2 limes
salt and pepper

SERVES 4

Place the stock in a saucepan and add the peeled sweet potatoes and half of the coriander/cilantro. Simmer until the sweet potato is soft.

Add the maple syrup, soy sauce and lime juice and season with salt and pepper to taste. Add the remaining coriander/cilantro and blitz in a blender or food processor until the soup is smooth, or use a stick blender.

Pour the soup into four bowls, garnish with a little fresh coriander/cilantro and serve straight away.

CHICKEN & GINGER BROTH

This is soup for the soul – ginger is said to have healing properties – and I always find a bowl of this soup a great pick-me-up when I am feeling under the weather. You can use chicken breast here, but I prefer the deeper flavour that comes from thigh meat.

500 g/1 lb. 2 oz. skinless, boneless chicken thighs
2.5-cm/1-in. piece of ginger, peeled and sliced into very thin julienne strips
6 spring onions/scallions, chopped, plus an extra 2 to serve
1 litre/4 cups chicken stock
1 tablespoon soy sauce
40 ml/2½ tablespoons mirin (sweet rice wine)

SERVES 4

Place the chicken thighs, ginger and spring onions/scallions in a saucepan with the stock, soy sauce and mirin and bring to a simmer. Simmer the soup over a gentle heat for about 30–40 minutes until the chicken is cooked and the soup has a strong chicken flavour.

Pass the soup through a fine-mesh sieve/strainer lined with muslin/cheesecloth to remove any impurities. Remove the chicken from the sieve/strainer and set aside.

Place the stock back in the saucepan with the cooked spring onions/scallions and ginger pieces from the sieve/strainer, leaving the impurities behind.

Blitz the soup quickly using a stick blender, or blitz it briefly in a blender or food processor, to blend some of the spring onion/scallion and ginger, but do not blitz for very long as you still want some pieces in the soup. Cut the chicken into bite-sized pieces and return to the saucepan.

Slice the additional two spring onions/scallions on the diagonal and add to the saucepan. Simmer the soup for 5 minutes until really hot, then divide between four bowls and serve straight away.

PRAWN/SHRIMP LAKSA SOUP

Laksa is a wonderfully fragrant broth from South Asia – it is popular in many Asian countries and each country has its own distinct recipe. This version is made with prawns/shrimp, but you could add cooked chicken or, for a vegetarian version, (bell) peppers and baby corn. Laksa paste is available in supermarkets and adds a delicate fragrance to this soup.

1 tablespoon coconut oil or vegetable oil
3 garlic cloves, finely sliced
1 red chilli/chile, finely sliced
2.5-cm/1-in. piece of ginger, peeled and finely sliced
2 tablespoons laksa paste
400 ml/1¾ cups coconut milk
700 ml/3 cups chicken stock
1 teaspoon tomato purée/paste
freshly squeezed juice of 2 limes
1 tablespoon sugar
30 g/1 oz. fresh coriander/cilantro, plus extra to garnish
20 raw king prawns/jumbo shrimp, tails on
140 g/5 oz. fine egg noodles
150 g/5½ oz. beansprouts
200 g/7 oz. choi sum or pak choi/bok choy

SERVES 4–5

Heat the coconut oil in a wok or large frying pan/skillet and add the garlic slices, chilli/chile and ginger and fry for a few minutes until the garlic is lightly golden brown. Add the laksa paste to the pan and fry for a few minutes.

Add the coconut milk, stock and tomato purée/paste to the pan together with the lime juice, sugar and coriander/cilantro. Simmer for about 20 minutes to allow the flavours to infuse.

Meanwhile, cut along the back of each prawn (this will help them to open up on cooking) and remove the black vein.

Shortly before you are ready to serve, add the egg noodles, beansprouts and prawns/shrimp to the soup. Simmer until the prawns/shrimp turn completely pink and the noodles are soft. A few minutes after adding the prawns/shrimp to the pan, add the choi sum or pak choi/bok choi (these will cook very quickly) and simmer until wilted (which should be about the same time as the prawns/shrimp are cooked).

Serve in bowls, making sure the prawns/shrimp are evenly distributed between your guests, topping each bowl with some extra fresh coriander/cilantro.

MATZO BALL CHICKEN SOUP

Matzo ball dough has one of the most comforting smells I know – with wheat biscuit meal and a hint of cinnamon, made rich with schmaltz (rendered chicken fat). If anyone is ever ill in our family, this is the recipe I turn to as a 'home-made penicillin'! You can make schmaltz yourself using the method in this recipe, but it is available to buy in good delicatessens.

1.5-kg/3¼-lb. whole chicken
2 sticks/ribs celery, sliced
6 carrots, peeled and cut into rings
2 bay leaves
10 peppercorns
1 chicken stock pot or cube (optional)
dill, to garnish (optional)

FOR THE MATZO BALLS
125 g/4½ oz. matzo meal
125 ml/½ cup sparkling water
½ teaspoon ground cinnamon
4 eggs, beaten
2 tablespoons schmaltz (see recipe method)
salt and pepper

SERVES 4–6

If you are making your own schmaltz, you need to start this recipe at least the day before you want to serve the soup. Place the chicken in a large pot and cover with water. Add the celery, half of the carrots, the bay leaves and peppercorns, and the chicken stock pot or cube (you can omit this if you prefer, but it helps to enhance the flavour of the soup). Simmer the chicken in the broth for about 1½ hours. Remove the chicken from the pot, reserving the stock. When cool enough to handle, remove the chicken meat from the bones and store in the fridge, covered, until ready to serve. Discard the chicken carcass.

Strain the stock through a fine-mesh sieve/strainer lined with muslin/cheesecloth into a container. Leave to cool, then store in the fridge overnight. Once chilled, the fat will have set on top of the stock. Remove the fat from the top of the stock – this is your schmaltz. There should be about 2 tablespoons schmaltz, which can be used to make the matzo balls, although if you want to speed up the process (as the matzo balls are best soaked overnight) then use store-bought schmaltz and reserve this schmaltz for another recipe.

For the matzo balls, mix the matzo meal in a bowl with the sparkling water, ground cinnamon, beaten eggs and schmaltz and season well with salt and pepper. Cover the bowl and place in the fridge for at least 6 hours, or preferably overnight, to allow the matzo meal to absorb the liquid.

When you are ready to prepare the soup, roll the matzo mixture into small balls, about the size of a whole walnut. Return the stock (with the schmaltz removed) to a saucepan. Bring the stock to the boil, then add the remaining carrots, the reserved chicken (cut into pieces) and the matzo balls. Reduce the heat and simmer for about 45 minutes. Remove a matzo ball and cut in half to see whether it is cooked – there should be no dark area in the centre.

Taste the soup for seasoning and then serve straight away, making sure each bowl has an even distribution of carrots, chicken and matzo balls. Garnish with dill fronds, if you like.

CHAPTER 4

SOUPS FOR SUMMER

SPRING VEGETABLE BROTH

Making consommé can seem daunting, even to chefs, as the perfect bowl needs to be crystal clear. No need to worry though, as this recipe is simplicity itself. It looks so pretty with asparagus tips and peas floating in it and every spoonful is full of the fresh taste of Spring.

1 large tomato, quartered
2 carrots, peeled and chopped
1 large leek, chopped
1 stick/rib of celery, trimmed and chopped
1 garlic clove, chopped
1 onion, quartered
75 ml/5 tablespoons Noilly Prat vermouth or sherry
1 tablespoon chopped fresh mint
1 sprig of fresh tarragon
2 teaspoons Worcestershire sauce
100 g/1 cup asparagus tips
100 g/generous ¾ cup shelled broad/fava beans
50 g/generous ⅓ cup frozen petit pois or peas
salt and pepper
toasted brioche, topped with cream cheese and feta and sprinkled with mint and lemon zest, to serve (optional)

SERVES 4

Place 1 litre/4 cups of water in a large saucepan and add the tomato, carrots, leek and celery with the garlic and onion. Season with salt and pepper. Add the Noilly Prat, mint and tarragon and bring to the boil. Reduce the heat and simmer over a low heat for about 30–40 minutes until the vegetables are all soft and the liquid has reduced.

Strain through a fine-mesh sieve/strainer. Do not press down on the vegetables, as this can add impurities to the soup. The soup should be very clear. Stir in the Worcestershire sauce and return the soup to the saucepan over a low heat. Add the asparagus, broad/fava beans and petit pois and simmer for about 5 minutes until the asparagus is just cooked. Taste for seasoning, adding more salt and pepper if needed.

Pour the soup into four bowls and serve with toasted brioche slices, topped with whipped cream cheese and feta and a sprinkling of chopped mint and lemon zest, if you like.

The soup will store for up to 3 days in the refrigerator, but cook the asparagus, broad/fava beans and peas just before serving.

STRAWBERRY GAZPACHO

My wonderful publisher and friend Julia Charles loves gazpacho and we often eat it in my garden in the sunshine when she comes to visit. It is perfect on hot days as it is so refreshing. I like to serve with something suitably summery, like tapenade-topped toasts with flavoursome toppings, such as feta, serrano ham, black olives and pickled peppers .

5 plum tomatoes
3 roasted red (bell) peppers in brine (such as Karyatis)
250 g/9 oz. strawberries
1 cucumber
2 spring onions/scallions
½ bulb fennel
a handful of fresh basil
½ teaspoon smoked paprika
30 ml/2 tablespoons white wine vinegar
75 ml/5 tablespoons olive oil, plus extra to drizzle
salt and pepper
toasted baguette slices, with your choice of toppings, to serve (optional)

SERVES 4

Cut the tomatoes in half and scoop out the seeds with a small spoon, then roughly chop the flesh. Chop the preserved (bell) peppers and place in a bowl with the tomatoes.

Reserve a few of the strawberries for the garnish, then hull and chop the remainder and add to the bowl with the tomatoes.

Trim the ends of the cucumber and peel off the skin with a swivel vegetable peeler. Cut the cucumber in half lengthways and deseed using a teaspoon. Set aside a little for the garnish, then chop the remainder and add to the bowl.

Trim the ends from the spring onions/scallions and fennel and roughly chop. Add to the bowl together with the basil, paprika, vinegar and olive oil. Season with salt and pepper, cover and chill in the refrigerator for 3 hours or overnight.

Blitz the soup to a smooth purée in a blender or food processor. Taste for seasoning, adding a little more salt and pepper if needed.

To serve, pour the soup into bowls or glasses. Finely chop the reserved strawberries and cucumber and place a little in the centre of each serving. Drizzle with a little olive oil, add a sprinkling of black pepper and serve straight away with some toasted and topped baguette slices, if you like.

CLAM CHOWDER

I have fond memories of eating clam chowder at a seafood restaurant in Boston, where everyone sat together on long tables. It was a fun evening and the soup was delicious. Clam chowder is very rich and really needs very little on the side, so if you do want to serve an accompaniment, go for something light and refreshing like a salad- and cream cheese-topped crispbread.

1 kg/2 lb. 4 oz. fresh clams
150 ml/⅔ cup Noilly Prat vermouth
500 g/1 lb. 2 oz. white potatoes, peeled and cut into small pieces
200 g/7 oz. diced pancetta
1 tablespoon olive oil
1 onion, sliced
30 g/2 tablespoons butter
2 tablespoons plain/all-purpose flour
250 ml/1 cup milk, plus extra if needed
250 ml/1 cup double/heavy cream
salt and pepper
salad-topped crispbreads, to serve (optional)

SERVES 4

This recipe uses fresh clams and it is important to cook them carefully to ensure that you do not use any dead clams. (If you prefer, you can substitute canned clams in the US, but these are not readily available in the UK.) Rinse the shells and check that they all close when tapped (discard any that remain open).

Place the clams in a pan with 250 ml/1 cup water and the Noilly Prat and cook for 6–8 minutes. The clam shells should open. Remove all opened clams from the pan and cook the remaining clams for a further 2–3 minutes. Discard any clams that remain closed. Remove the clams from their shells and set aside in the refrigerator while you prepare the soup. Reserve the cooking liquid but strain it through a fine-mesh sieve/strainer to remove any impurities.

Cook the potatoes in plenty of salted boiling water until just soft. Drain and set aside.

In a large saucepan, cook the pancetta in the olive oil until crisp. Remove from the pan, then add the onion to the pan and fry until it is soft and translucent. Return the pancetta to the pan with the potatoes and cook for a few minutes more. Add the butter to the pan and allow to melt, then stir in the flour and cook for a few minutes.

Add the clam cooking liquid to the pan, straining it again before adding. Simmer for a few minutes, then add the milk and cream and season to taste. If the soup is too thick, add a little more milk or water to loosen. Simmer for 10 minutes, then stir through the reserved clams.

Spoon the soup into four bowls and serve straight away with salad- and cream cheese-topped crispbreads, if you like.

CHILLED BROAD/FAVA BEAN, PEA & MINT SOUP

This soup is perfect for a summer supper party and is so refreshing served chilled. It can also be served warm, topped with grated cheese for a warming yet refreshing soup. It has a vibrant green colour and is lovely swirled with cream to finish. To make the soup as smooth as possible, pass the soup through a moulin or a fine-mesh sieve/strainer.

15 g/1 tablespoon butter
1 tablespoon olive oil
1 onion, finely chopped
1 garlic clove, finely chopped
40 ml/2½ tablespoons brandy
200 g/1½ cups frozen peas
200 g/1½ cups frozen broad/ fava beans
1 litre/4 cups vegetable or chicken stock
4 large sprigs of fresh mint
100 ml/⅓ cup plus 1 tablespoon double/heavy cream, plus extra to serve (optional)
salt and pepper

SERVES 4

Heat the butter and olive oil in a saucepan over a medium heat and sauté the onion until soft and translucent. Add the garlic and fry until lightly golden brown.

Add the brandy and heat for a few minutes to cook off the alcohol. Add the peas, broad/fava beans and stock together with the mint and bring to the boil. Reduce the heat and simmer for about 10 minutes until the peas and beans are soft. Remove a large spoonful of peas and beans to reserve for garnish.

Blend the soup in a blender or food processor, or using stick blender, until smooth and then pass through the moulin or a fine-mesh sieve/ strainer to remove the pea and bean skins. If passing through a sieve/ strainer, use a rubber spatula to push it through.

Season with salt and pepper. If you want to make the soup richer, stir in the double/heavy cream. Chill in the fridge until you are ready to serve.

To serve, pour the cold soup into four bowls and finish with a swirl of double/heavy cream and some freshly ground black pepper, plus a sprinkle of the reserved peas and beans. For an extra chilled soup, add an ice cube when you serve.

CORN, LIME & CHILLI SOUP

One of the things I love to serve is barbecued/grilled corn with chilli/chile and lime butter – it has such a zesty tang with fire from the chilli/chile and the smoky coals and is perfect for summer days. This soup is inspired by those sunshine flavours. You could easily substitute fresh corn, but, for ease, this recipe uses frozen or canned corn which I always have in my freezer or storecupboard as standbys.

30 g/2 tablespoons butter
1 onion, finely chopped
1–2 red chillies/chiles, deseeded and finely sliced, to taste, plus extra to garnish
1 garlic clove, finely chopped
400 g/14 oz. frozen or canned sweetcorn/corn kernels, drained and rinsed if canned
1 litre/4 cups chicken or vegetable stock
zest and freshly squeezed juice of 2 limes, plus extra to taste, if needed
250 g/9 oz. white potatoes, peeled and cubed
salt and pepper
crème fraîche or sour cream, to serve

SERVES 4

Add the butter and onion to a large saucepan over a medium heat and sauté for about 5 minutes until the onion softens and starts to caramelize. Add the chilli(es)/chile(s) and garlic to the pan and cook for a further 2 minutes. Use the amount of chilli/chile that you feel comfortable with – one is fine, but if you like hot and spicy, use a second.

Place the frozen or drained sweetcorn/corn kernels in the pan and cook for a further 5 minutes. Add the stock, lime juice and potato and simmer for 15–20 minutes until the potato is soft.

Blend the soup in a blender or food processor, or with a stick blender, until smooth, and then pass through a moulin or fine-mesh sieve/strainer to remove the corn skins.

Season with salt and pepper and add a little more lime juice to taste, if you wish.

Pour the soup into four bowls and serve hot with a spoonful of sour cream or crème fraîche swirled in. Finish with a little finely sliced chilli/chile and a sprinkling of pepper.

COURGETTE/ZUCCHINI LEMON YOGURT SOUP

When I was at university, we had a supper club and would all take turns to make a course for our dinners. This was a soup made by my friend Tina, which was so tasty I am still making it many years later. It has a light and refreshing flavour and is slightly sour with the lemon and yogurt. Make sure that the temperature is low when you add the yogurt, as it can split if the soup is too hot.

1 onion, finely chopped
2 tablespoons olive oil
1 garlic clove, finely chopped
300 g/10½ oz. courgettes/zucchini, green or yellow, coarsely grated
1 litre/4 cups chicken or vegetable stock
1 egg
250 ml/1 cup natural/plain yogurt
freshly squeezed juice of 2 lemons
1 tablespoon chopped fresh tarragon, plus extra to serve
salt and pepper
Garlic Croûtons (see page 10), to serve

SERVES 4

In a large saucepan, heat the oil over a medium heat and fry the onion until soft and translucent. Add the garlic and fry until lightly golden brown. Add half of the grated courgette/zucchini and the stock and simmer for 10–15 minutes until the courgette/zucchini is soft.

In a bowl, beat the egg with the yogurt. Add a ladleful of the hot stock from the soup and whisk together to warm the yogurt before adding to the soup (this will prevent it from splitting). Add the lemon juice and tarragon to the egg and yogurt mixture, and then whisk it all into the soup. Blend the soup in a blender or food processor until smooth, or use a stick blender.

Return the soup to the pan and add the remaining courgette/zucchini. Simmer for a few minutes, then pour the soup into four bowls and serve topped with extra chopped fresh tarragon, a sprinkling of black pepper and some garlic croûtons.

AVGOLEMONO (LEMON & CHICKEN SOUP)

This Greek soup is a complete meal in itself and needs no accompaniment. As it cooks, the aromas transport me to islands with white and blue painted houses. The lemon and chicken work perfectly together and the rice gives the soup a richness and a consistency akin to a very soft risotto.

30 g/2 tablespoons butter
1 onion, finely chopped
2 garlic cloves, finely chopped
170 g/1 cup white rice
250 ml/1 cup white wine
1 litre/4 cups chicken stock
2 cooked chicken breasts, sliced, any bones and skin removed
1 large carrot, peeled and cut into rings or rounds
2 eggs
freshly squeezed juice of 1 lemon
500 ml/2 cups hot water
salt and pepper
fresh flat-leaf parsley, to serve

SERVES 4–6

Heat the butter in a large saucepan over a medium heat and add the onion. Sauté until soft and translucent, then add the garlic and fry until lightly golden brown.

Add the rice to the pan and cook in the butter for a few minutes, seasoning well with salt and pepper. Add the white wine and heat for a few minutes to cook off the alcohol and to intensify the flavour. Add the chicken stock, chicken pieces and carrot and simmer for about 20–30 minutes until the rice is cooked and the carrot is soft.

In a separate heatproof bowl, beat together the eggs and lemon juice. Add a ladleful of the hot soup from the pan to the bowl and whisk in. Add the egg mixture to the pan to thicken the soup. Add a little more water if the soup becomes too thick.

Serve straight away – do not return to the heat after adding the egg. Pour into bowls and top with fresh parsley and some black pepper.

TOMATO WATER WITH CRACKLING STRAWS

This is a dish that I made on MasterChef. The portions are small but bursting with flavour and are ideal served with salty crackling straws to offset the sweetness of the tomatoes.

16 large, very ripe and juicy tomatoes, roughly chopped
1 tablespoon caster/granulated sugar
250 ml/1 cup white wine
salt and pepper

FOR THE CRACKLING STRAWS
30 x 10-cm/12 x 4-in piece of pork skin, all fat removed
olive oil, to drizzle
sea salt

baking sheet, oiled

SERVES 4

Place the tomatoes in a saucepan (including all the juice) with the sugar and white wine and season well with lots of salt and pepper (the seasoning will not be as strong when chilled, so make sure you add plenty of seasoning). Bring to the boil then reduce the heat and simmer for about 5 minutes.

Place a piece of muslin/cheesecloth in a fine-mesh sieve/strainer and strain the liquid three times to remove the colour – you want the soup to be as clear as possible. Pour into shot glasses and chill in the fridge.

To make the crackling straws, preheat the oven to 200°C (400°F) Gas 6. Cut the pork skin into long thin strips with scissors.

Line up the strips of pork skin on the oiled baking sheet and sprinkle over rock salt. Place another baking sheet on top and weigh it down with something heavy and ovenproof (a heavy casserole dish is ideal for this) so that the crackling bakes straight. Bake in the preheated oven for 15–20 minutes until the crackling is golden brown.

Serve a crackling straw in each glass of chilled soup.

AJO BLANCO (CHILLED ALMOND SOUP)

This creamy garlic soup is a delight served extra chilled. It's best to pour the soup over an ice cube as you serve, as this will make the temperature perfect. Always use blanched almonds for this recipe. You can use regular blanched almonds, but I find that Marcona almonds have the best flavour for this soup. Serving with green grapes adds a refreshing sweetness. This soup is best prepared ahead of time, so that it is properly chilled, which makes it an ideal dish for a dinner party, with no last-minute preparation other than pouring and garnishing.

70 g/2½ oz. stale bread (crusts removed), cut into cubes
500 ml/2 cups milk
150 g/1¼ cups blanched Marcona almonds
2 garlic cloves, cut into thin slices
40 ml/2½ tablespoons olive oil
40 ml/2½ tablespoons sherry vinegar
salt and pepper
avocado oil or extra-virgin olive oil, to serve
green grapes, halved, to serve

SERVES 4

Place the bread in a bowl and soak for 15 minutes in 125 ml/½ cup of the milk.

Reserve a few of the almonds for the garnish, then place the remaining almonds in a blender or food processor with the garlic, olive oil and vinegar. Blend until you have a smooth paste, scraping down the sides of the bowl between blending. Add the bread and soaking milk and blitz again. Add 250 ml/1 cup of the milk, pouring it in gradually, and blitz again until the soup is a smooth paste. Scrape down the sides again and then add the final 125ml/½ cup of the milk, together with salt and pepper to taste. Blend for a few minutes further to make sure the soup has a very smooth texture and is pourable. You can add a little extra milk if the consistency is too thick.

Pass through a fine-mesh sieve/strainer, pressing it through with a rubber spatula to make sure the soup is as smooth as possible. Chill in the fridge for a few hours.

When you are ready to serve, place an ice cube in each of the bowls and pour the soup over. This will ensure the soup is extra chilled. Drizzle with a little avocado oil and serve straight away with some sliced grapes and the reserved almonds.

LETTUCE SOUP

This soup is perfect for keen allotment owners who end up with a glut of lettuces in the summer. It is delicious hot, but also works well as a chilled soup for hot days. It surprisingly tastes very much like pea soup without a pea in sight. If you don't have cream, milk works well as a substitute. You can also omit this from the recipe if you want to make a vegan soup – if so, use olive oil rather than butter and vegetable stock in place of chicken.

15 g/1 tablespoon butter
1 onion, finely chopped
2 garlic cloves, finely chopped
1 lettuce, such as iceberg or Cos/Romaine
1 large potato, peeled and cut into cubes
1 litre/4 cups chicken stock
3–4 sprigs of fresh mint, plus extra to garnish
200 ml/¾ cup double/heavy cream
salt and pepper
Welsh Rarebit Toasts (see page 11) or Garlic Croûtons (see page 10), to serve

SERVES 4

Heat the butter in a saucepan and sauté the onion and garlic over a gentle heat until soft and translucent.

Trim the stalk from the lettuce and remove any outer leaves with blemishes. Cut the lettuce into chunks and rinse. Add the lettuce to the pan together with the potato, stock and mint and simmer for around 20 minutes until the potato is soft.

Blend in a blender or food processor, or use a stick blender, until smooth. Return the soup to the pan and add the cream. Heat gently and season with salt and pepper.

Pour into four bowls and add a sprinkling of black pepper and some fresh mint to garnish. Serve straight away with Welsh rarebit toasts or garlic croûtons.

FRENCH FISH SOUP WITH AÏOLI

1 tablespoon olive oil
30 g/2 tablespoons butter
1 onion, finely chopped
2 sticks/ribs celery, finely sliced
1 carrot, peeled and cut into very small cubes
½ bulb fennel, trimmed and finely sliced
2 garlic cloves, peeled and finely chopped
2 star anise
grated zest of 1 small orange
about 20 cherry tomatoes, halved
125 ml/½ cup Noilly Prat vermouth
250 ml/1 cup white wine
500 ml/2 cups fish stock
a pinch of saffron
2 bay leaves
500 g/1 lb. 2 oz. live mussels
10 raw large prawns/jumbo shrimp
200 g/7 oz. white fish such as sea bass fillets, deboned
2 tablespoons chopped fresh flat-leaf parsley
salt and pepper

FOR THE AÏOLI
1 heaped teaspoon Dijon mustard
2 garlic cloves, peeled and finely sliced
2 egg yolks
75 ml/5 tablespoons vegetable oil
75 ml/5 tablespoons olive oil
freshly squeezed juice of ½ lemon

SERVES 4–6

On MasterChef fish soup was an invention test that became my nemesis as we had to make it without any recipe, and I was petrified. I am pleased to say that since MasterChef I have overcome my fear of this soup and it is now a family favourite.

First, make the aïoli. Place the mustard, garlic and egg yolks in a blender or food processor and blitz to a smooth paste. Scrape down the sides and blitz again. With the blades still running, slowly pour in the vegetable oil and then the olive oil. The aïoli should emulsify and be thick. Stir in lemon juice to taste and season with salt and pepper. Set aside while you make the soup.

In a large sauté pan, heat the olive oil and half of the butter over a gentle heat. Add the onion, celery, carrot, fennel and garlic, together with the star anise and orange zest, and simmer over a gentle heat until all the vegetables become soft. It is worth taking the time to cook slowly as it will enhance the flavour of the soup. Add the remaining butter to the pan as you continue to sweat the vegetables down.

Add the halved tomatoes to the pan with the vermouth and white wine and simmer for a few minutes to cook off the alcohol. Add the fish stock, saffron, bay leaves and 250 ml/1 cup water to the pan and simmer for 30 minutes, adding more water if needed. Taste the soup and season with salt and pepper. The soup should have a good strong flavour.

Clean the mussels, discarding any that do not close when tapped and removing any beards. Rinse well.

Add the mussels, prawns/shrimp and white fish to the pan and cover with a lid. Simmer for about 5–10 minutes until the fish is cooked and the mussels are open, and the prawns/shrimp are pink all over. Stir the pan halfway through cooking to ensure that everything is cooked. Discard any mussels that are still closed.

Distribute the fish, prawns/shrimp and mussels evenly between your bowls and pour over the soup (discarding the star anise). If the soup has evaporated too much during cooking, add more water to the pan. Sprinkle with fresh parsley and serve straight away with the aïoli, on slices of toast or just spooned into the soup. It is delicious either way.

CHAPTER 5

SOMETHING SPECIAL

VELVETY CHEESE & BEER SOUP

This is an indulgent soup with a fiery kick. It is rich with cream and cheese and has delicious, and slightly unexpected, undertones of hops from the beer. It is served here with a quesadilla (filled fried tortilla) for dunking, but it works equally well served with some crusty sourdough on the side. To make a gluten-free version of this soup, use a gluten-free beer

2 onions, chopped
2 carrots, peeled and chopped
1 garlic clove, peeled and chopped
30 g/2 tablespoons butter
1 tablespoon olive oil
1 heaped tablespoon plain/all-purpose flour
400 ml/scant 1¾ cups beer
600 ml/2½ cups chicken or vegetable stock
1 teaspoon creamed horseradish sauce
½–1 teaspoon hot sauce, to taste
250 ml/1 cup double/heavy cream
2 tablespoons sour cream
100 g/scant ½ cup cream cheese
125 g/1⅓ cups grated Cheddar
salt and pepper
quesadilla of your choice, to serve (optional)

SERVES 4

In a large saucepan, heat the butter and oil over a gentle heat and add the onions, carrots and garlic. Sauté until the onions are soft and translucent. Take care the garlic does not burn and stir all the time.

Add the flour to the pan and cook for a minute, then add the beer and stock to the pan and simmer for about 5 minutes.

Add the horseradish, hot sauce, double/heavy cream, sour cream, cream cheese and grated cheddar cheese. Stir until all the cheese has melted.

Blitz the soup in a blender or food processor until very smooth, then return to the pan. You can also use a stick blender. Taste for seasoning and add a little salt and pepper if needed.

Pour the soup into four bowls, sprinkle with extra black pepper and serve with a quesadilla, if you like.

LANGOUSTINE BISQUE

This is a rich soup with a really intense flavour, which comes from roasting the shells of the langoustines before putting them into the soup. To make a more substantial meal, serve it with buttered seafood cocktail rolls.

1 kg/2 lb. whole langoustines
2 tablespoons olive oil
2 onions, finely chopped
1 garlic clove, finely chopped
1 stick/rib celery, chopped
4 carrots, peeled and finely chopped
2 sprigs of fresh thyme
60 g/½ stick butter
75 ml/5 tablespoons brandy, plus a dash for the soup
160 ml/¾ cup Noilly Prat vermouth
2 large tomatoes, quartered
1 tablespoon tomato purée/paste
400-g/14-oz. can tomatoes
500 ml/2 cups fish stock
freshly squeezed juice of 1 lemon, plus lemon wedges to serve
200 ml/generous ¾ cup double/heavy cream
salt and pepper
chopped fresh parsley and chives, to garnish
seafood cocktail rolls, to serve (optional)

SERVES 4

Bring a large stockpot of salted water to the boil. Add the langoustines and simmer for about 5 minutes until cooked (the meat under the tail should have turned white).

Place into cold water to chill and then remove the head and tail, peel the shell from the body and remove the black intestinal tract. Reserve the shells. Chill the langoustine flesh until needed.

Preheat the oven to 200°C (400°F) Gas 6.

Place the langoustine heads and shells in a large roasting pan, drizzle with 1 tablespoon of the olive oil and season. Roast in the preheated oven for 20–30 minutes until the shells turn light golden brown.

Meanwhile, add the onions, garlic, celery and carrots to a large saucepan with the remaining 1 tablespoon olive oil and the thyme. Gently sauté for 10–15 minutes until the vegetables soften. Remove from the pan and set aside.

Tip the roasted shells into a clean saucepan, add 50 g/3½ tablespoons of the butter and fry for a few minutes over a medium heat. Add the brandy and Noilly Prat and cook for 2 minutes. Add the fresh tomatoes along with the onion, garlic, celery and carrot mixture, the tomato purée/paste, canned tomatoes, fish stock and 1 litre/4 cups of water. Season with salt and pepper. Cook for 1½ hours over a gentle heat.

Pass the soup through a fine-mesh sieve/strainer or piece of muslin. cheesecloth in batches.

Return the soup to the pan and add the lemon juice and cream. To finish the soup add the remaining 10 g/2 teaspoons butter, an extra dash of brandy and heat through.

Pour the soup into four bowls and garnish with chopped fresh parsley and chives. If you are serving with seafood rolls, use the cooked langoustines for the rolls. If you are not serving seafood rolls, add the langoustines to the soup for an extra touch of luxury.

LASAGNE SOUP

Who doesn't love a lasagne? It is one of the most popular dishes. This soup takes all of the elements – rich beef Bolognese, creamy white sauce, mozzarella and lasagne pasta sheets – and makes them into a satisfying soup. You can use soup pasta rather than lasagne if you prefer.

1 tablespoon olive oil
400 g/14 oz. minced/ground beef (low fat)
1 tablespoon Worcestershire sauce
15 g/1 tablespoon butter
1 onion, finely chopped
2 garlic cloves, finely chopped
1 large carrot, peeled and grated
400-g/14-oz. can chopped tomatoes
250 ml/1 cup red wine
70 g/5 tablespoons tomato purée/paste
1 litre/4 cups beef stock
4 sheets of lasagne pasta
1 ball of mozzarella (about 150 g/5½ oz.)
salt and pepper
fresh basil leaves, to serve
freshly grated Parmesan, to serve

FOR THE CHEESE SAUCE
60 g/4 tablespoons butter
50 g/heaping ⅓ cup plain/all-purpose flour
300 ml/1¼ cups milk
freshly grated nutmeg
100 g/1 cup plus 2 tablespoons grated Cheddar
50 g/⅔ cup grated Parmesan

SERVES 6

Heat the olive oil in a large saucepan over a medium heat, add the beef and fry until it is all browned and cooked through, stirring all the time to ensure it does not stick. Add the Worcestershire sauce to the pan and cook for a further minute, then season well with salt and pepper. Remove the beef from the pan using a slotted spoon and drain on paper towels to remove as much fat as possible. Set aside.

Melt the butter in a frying pan/skillet and fry the onion over a gentle heat until soft and translucent. Add the garlic and sauté until lightly golden brown. Add the carrot and sauté for a few minutes until it starts to soften, then return the meat to the pan and add the tomatoes, wine, tomato purée/paste and beef stock. Season with salt and pepper and simmer for about 30 minutes until the sauce thickens. It will still be a very liquid soupy consistency, unlike a traditional ragù.

Break the lasagne sheets into pieces and add to the soup, adding more stock or water if the soup is too thick. Simmer for about 10 minutes ntil the pasta is soft.

Meanwhile, prepare the cheese sauce. Melt the butter in a clean saucepan over a gentle heat and add the flour, whisking all the time, to form a roux. Cook for a few minutes. Little by little, add the milk, whisking constantly, until you have a thick but pourable sauce. Season with a good grate of nutmeg, salt and pepper and then add the grated Cheddar and Parmesan. Whisk until melted. Remove from the heat and cover the surface with a sheet of clingfilm/plastic wrap to prevent a skin from forming. Keep warm.

When you are ready to serve, pour the hot soup into bowls, then cut the mozzarella into small pieces and add to the soup. Make sure that each bowl has some of the pasta in it. Pour over some of the cheese sauce and top with fresh basil and freshly grated Parmesan to serve.

MASSAMAN POTATO SOUP

Massaman curry is a Thai delight – a mild but flavour-packed curry bursting with peanuts and potatoes and rich with coconut milk. This soup is inspired by that curry and trips to Thailand. Traditionally a Massaman curry is made with beef, but this is my vegetarian interpretation.

1 tablespoon olive oil
1 onion, finely chopped
1 garlic clove, finely chopped
1 tablespoon massaman curry paste
450 g/1 lb. potatoes, peeled and cut into 2.5-cm/1-in. cubes
2 tablespoons peanut butter
200 ml/¾ cup coconut milk
600 ml/2½ cups vegetable stock
freshly squeezed juice of 1–2 limes, to taste
1 tablespoon pure maple syrup
salt and pepper
salted peanuts, finely chopped, to serve
red chilli/chile slices, to serve

SERVES 4

Heat the olive oil in a saucepan over a gentle heat and sauté the onion until it is soft and translucent and starts to caramelize. Add the garlic and cook for a further few minutes, taking care it does not burn. Add the massaman paste and cook for a further 1–2 minutes.

Add the potatoes, peanut butter, coconut milk and stock and simmer until the potatoes are very soft. The potatoes will break up and the soup will thicken.

Add the lime juice and maple syrup and season with salt and pepper. Although you can blend the soup, I prefer to leave the potatoes in chunks to add texture to the soup.

Pour the soup into bowls and sprinkle with chopped peanuts, chilli/chile slices and some black pepper to serve.

CARROT & STAR ANISE SOUP

My friends Lucy and David made wonderful star anise-roasted carrots for lunch one day, and that delicious meal was the inspiration for this soup. It is so easy to prepare as it is baked in the oven in one pan – no hassle, just baking then blending – and the result is a sweet, delicious soup with hints of aniseed. Serve with carrot crisps and crème fraîche for a perfect treat.

800 g/1 lb. 12 oz. carrots, peeled
3 whole star anise
1 litre/4 cups chicken or vegetable stock
60 ml/4 tablespoons pure maple syrup
100 g/7 tablespoons butter
olive oil, to drizzle
salt and pepper
crème fraîche or sour cream, to serve

SERVES 4

Preheat the oven to 180°C (350°F) Gas 4.

Set aside 1 carrot for making the carrot crisps, then slice all the other carrots and place in a large roasting tray. Season well with salt and pepper. Add the star anise, stock, maple syrup and butter to the pan. Bake uncovered in the oven for 30 minutes until the carrots are tender and a knife cuts them easily.

Remove the star anise and discard. Carefully pour the liquid into a blender or food processor and blend until smooth. If you are using a stick blender, you may find it easiest to pour the carrots and stock mixture into a large saucepan and blend it in there – you can blend it in the roasting pan, but it may splash!

Whilst the soup is cooking prepare the carrot crisps. Using a swivel peeler or mandoline, cut very thin slices from the reserved carrot. Toss lightly in a drizzle of olive oil and season well with salt and pepper. Place the strips (stretching them out so that they are flat) on a baking sheet and bake for about 5–10 minutes until crisp, checking regularly as they can burn quickly.

Pour the soup into four bowls and serve hot with a dollop of crème fraîche or sour cream and the carrot crisps on top.

CARIBBEAN SWEET POTATO & COCONUT SOUP

Jerk paste has the most amazing fiery flavour and immediately transports me to Caribbean holidays. It is so versatile and can be used to flavour anything for the barbecue/outdoor grill, as well as stews or, as here, soups. It can be very fiery, so take care not to add too much, otherwise the soup can be overpoweringly hot.

2 tablespoons olive oil
1 onion, finely chopped
2 garlic cloves, finely chopped
1 teaspoon jerk paste
1 tablespoon tomato purée/paste
600–700 g/1 lb. 5 oz.–1 lb. 9 oz. sweet potato, peeled and cut into chunks
700 ml/scant 3 cups chicken or vegetable stock
400-ml/14-oz. can coconut milk
salt and pepper
toasted strips of coconut, to serve

SERVES 4–6

In a large saucepan, heat the oil over a gentle heat and add the onion. Fry until soft and translucent. Add the garlic and cook for a few minutes until it is lightly golden brown. Add the jerk paste and fry to infuse the flavours. How much depends on how hot you like your food. Jerk paste is generally very fiery so take care not to add too much unless you like very hot spices.

Add the tomato purée/paste and the sweet potatoes and cook for a few minutes more, then add the stock and the coconut milk. Simmer until the potatoes are soft; around 20–30 minutes.

Place the soup in a blender or food processor and blend until smooth, or use a stick blender. Season with salt and pepper to taste.

Serve hot with toasted coconut and some extra black pepper.

CELERIAC/CELERY ROOT & APPLE SOUP

Poor celeriac/celery root. It is not a pretty vegetable, but what it does have going for it is a delicious creamy texture and perfumed celery flavour. There are lots of ingredients you could add to this recipe – fry off some garlic and onion before you cook the soup base, add a glass of white wine, a few leeks – and all will taste good. However, I really do prefer the pared-back flavour of this soup, which just lets the celeriac/celery root shine through, with a little tartness from the apple to balance out the creaminess. If you like celery, then I have no doubt you will enjoy this soup. Top it with pickled apple batons to cut through the richness of the soup.

2 kg/4½ lb. celeriac/celery root, peeled and cut into cubes
3 green apples, peeled, cored and cut into quarters
1.5 litres/6 cups chicken or vegetable stock
250 ml/1 cup double/heavy cream or milk
30 g/2 tablespoons butter
salt and pepper
chopped fresh chervil or parsley, to garnish

FOR THE APPLE BATONS
freshly squeezed juice of 1 lemon
2 tablespoons cider or white wine vinegar
1 heaped tablespoon caster/granulated sugar
1 star anise
1 apple, cored

SERVES 4–6

Begin by preparing the pickling syrup for the apple batons. Heat the lemon juice, vinegar, sugar and star anise in a saucepan until the sugar has dissolved. Set aside to cool.

For the soup, place the cubed celeriac/celery root and apple wedges in a large saucepan with the stock and bring to the boil. Reduce to a simmer and cook over a gentle heat for 30–40 minutes until the celeriac/celery root is soft and cuts easily with a knife.

Add the cream and butter and stir until the butter melts. Blitz in a blender or food processor until smooth and silky, or use a stick blender.

When you are almost ready to serve, make the apple batons by cutting the cored apple into thin sticks – I like to leave the skin on as it looks pretty. Place the batons into the cooled pickling liquid and stir for a few minutes so they are completely covered. Do not leave the batons in the syrup for long, because they will become soft, and drain before using as garnish.

Serve the soup hot, topped with the apple batons and a little chopped fresh chervil or parsley.

SPICY AUBERGINE/EGGPLANT SOUP

Here, roasted, aubergine/eggplant takes on an amazingly rich flavour and becomes the perfect base for a soup. Roasted with sweet chillies/chiles and tomatoes, the soup is smoky and tangy. Top with swirls of pesto and yogurt for an extra special treat.

2 aubergine/eggplants, cut into 2.5-cm/1-in. cubes
3 small, sweet chillies/chiles, deseeded
20 small cherry tomatoes
3 tablespoons olive oil
1 litre/4 cups hot vegetable stock
salt and pepper
natural/plain yogurt, crème fraîche or sour cream, to serve

FOR THE PESTO DRIZZLE
1 tablespoon Homemade Pesto (see page 15 or use fresh store-bought)
1 tablespoon olive oil
freshly squeezed juice of 1 lemon

SERVES 4

Preheat the oven to 180°C (350°F) Gas 4.

Place the chopped aubergine/eggplant, chillies/chiles and tomatoes in a large roasting pan, drizzle with the olive oil and roast for 25–30 minutes until the aubergine/eggplant is golden brown and tender. Set aside a large spoonful of the vegetables for the garnish.

Pour the hot vegetable stock into the roasting pan and return the pan to the oven for another 10 minutes.

Whilst the vegetables are cooking, prepare the pesto drizzle by whisking together the pesto with the olive oil and lemon juice until you have a thin paste.

Remove the roasting pan from the oven, pour the contents of the pan into a blender or food processor and blitz until smooth and thick. If you are using a stick blender, you may find it easiest to pour the mixture into a large saucepan and blend it in there – you can blend it in the roasting pan, but it may splash!

Make sure that the soup is piping hot to serve, reheating it in a saucepan if necessary.

Pour the soup into bowls and serve with a swirl of yogurt, a few of the reserved vegetables and a drizzle of pesto dressing.

ROASTED PUMPKIN SOUP

Pumpkin soup is a classic to serve at Halloween or for Bonfire Night – it freezes well so you can prepare ahead and then just defrost and reheat on the day. For an extra spooky treat, why not serve in roasted pumpkin bowls – once the soup is eaten you can eat the bowl too. Small pumpkins and squashes work perfectly for this (see tip below).

1.3 kg/3 lb. pumpkin or butternut squash, peeled and roughly chopped
grated zest and freshly squeezed juice of 1 orange
1 teaspoon ground ginger
3 tablespoons olive oil
1 litre/4 cups chicken or vegetable stock
salt and pepper
double/heavy cream, to serve
Toasted Truffle Seed Mix or Savoury Granola (see page 13), to serve

SERVES 4

Preheat the oven to 180°C (350°F) Gas 4.

Place the chopped squash or pumpkin in a roasting pan and sprinkle over the orange zest and juice, ginger and olive oil. Roast in the preheated oven for 20–30 minutes until the squash/pumpkin is soft when you cut it with a knife.

Remove from the oven and place in a saucepan with the stock over a medium heat. Bring to the boil then reduce the heat and simmer for about 15 minutes. Blitz in a food processor or blender until the soup is smooth, or use a stick blender.

Pour the soup into four bowls and add a swirl of cream to each. Serve topped with toasted seeds or savoury granola.

Tip: If you are making the pumpkin shell bowls, scoop out the insides of 4 small pumpkins or the round end of 4 small butternut squashes so that there is a thin layer of flesh remaining on the skin. Use the flesh in the soup recipe above. Drizzle the shells with olive oil and season with salt and pepper and roast in the oven for 25–30 minutes until the flesh is soft but the pumpkin or squash bowl still holds its shape. Serve the soup in the roasted bowls.

MEXICAN TORTILLA SOUP

The delights of fried tortillas cannot be underestimated – it is my guilty pleasure and they go well with many types of soup. Served here with a rich tomato and chicken soup with spice, it's a complete meal in itself. I serve this soup topped with avocado, sour cream, cheese and diced fresh tomato.

1 onion, chopped
2 garlic cloves, finely sliced
1 tablespoon olive oil
1 red Romano pepper, deseeded and cut into large chunks
1 yellow (bell) pepper, deseeded and cut into large chunks
1 teaspoon sweet paprika
2 teaspoons chipotle paste
400-g/14-oz. can chopped tomatoes (or 400 g/14 oz. fresh, if you prefer)
70 g/5 tablespoons tomato purée/paste
1 litre/4 cups chicken stock
freshly squeezed juice of 2 limes
1 tablespoon pure maple syrup
25 g/1 oz. fresh coriander/cilantro, plus extra to garnish
8 chicken thighs, cooked
salt and pepper

FRIED TORTILLAS
4 large corn tortillas
a pinch of sweet paprika (optional)
vegetable oil, for frying

TO SERVE
1 ripe avocado, pitted and peeled
freshly squeezed juice of 1 lime
2 ripe tomatoes, deseeded, flesh finely diced
4–6 tablespoons sour cream
a handful of grated Cheddar

SERVES 4–6

For the soup, fry the onion and garlic in the oil in a large saucepan over a gentle heat until soft and translucent. Add the Romano pepper and (bell) pepper chunks and fry until they start to soften.

Add the paprika and chipotle paste to the pan and simmer for a few minutes to allow the flavours to infuse, then add the chopped tomatoes, tomato purée/paste and chicken stock. Season with salt pepper and simmer for about 30 minutes.

Add the lime juice, maple syrup and coriander/cilantro to the pan and simmer for a few minutes. Use a stick blender to blitz the soup until smooth, or blitz in a blender or food processor and then return to the pan. Cut the cooked chicken thighs into small strips and add to the pan. Simmer for about 15 minutes until the chicken is hot. Taste the soup for seasoning and add a little more salt, pepper or lime juice as needed.

Whilst the soup is cooking, prepare the tortillas. Fill a large frying pan/skillet with vegetable oil to a depth of 2 cm/¾ in. and place over a medium heat (or use a deep-fryer if you prefer). Cut the tortillas into strips about 10 cm/4 in. in length and 2 cm/¾ in. wide. Fry in batches until they lightly golden, turning them during cooking with a spatula to ensure even cooking. Remove from the pan and drain on paper towels. Sprinkle with salt and pepper (and a little paprika, if you wish).

Prepare the toppings for the soup. Cut the avocado into small cubes and sprinkle with the lime juice to prevent it discolouring. Cut the tomato flesh into small cubes.

When you are ready to serve, pour the hot soup into bowls. Top each bowl with some chopped avocado, chopped fresh tomato, a little soured cream and a sprinkle of grated cheese. Garnish with a little fresh coriander/cilantro and add a handful of the tortilla chips (or serve these on the side, if you wish). People love the tortilla chips, so I always prepare extra and am never left with any – they are totally moreish!

EGG RIBBON SOUP

This recipe is my take on the classic Chinese egg ribbon soup. It was inspired by a meal I had many years ago at L'Enclume (in the days before it held any Michelin star – it now holds three!) where we were served steaming hot and delicious broth at our table with a syringe filled with egg on the side. Guests piped the egg into the soup to make egg ribbons. It was such a novelty, and an interactive menu is always fun. You can do that with the eggs in the recipe, if you like – it is essential that the broth is piping hot so that the eggs cook. Alternatively, you can make the ribbons using a piping/pastry bag whilst cooking. Either way, this is a simple, fragrant and highly delicious soup. To make this soup extra luxurious, decorate with edible gold leaf and some caviar, ideal for a Chinese New Year Feast.

1 litre/4 cups chicken stock
2.5-cm/1-in. piece of ginger, peeled and cut into thin julienne strips
2 garlic cloves, finely sliced
1 tablespoon soy sauce
60 ml/4 tablespoons mirin (rice wine)
1 tablespoon cornflour/ cornstarch
1 egg, beaten
salt and pepper

TO SERVE
4 teaspoons caviar
a little gold leaf

piping/pastry bag fitted with a very fine nozzle/tip

SERVES 4

Place the chicken stock in a saucepan and bring to a simmer over a gentle heat, adding the ginger pieces and garlic. Simmer for about 15 minutes to allow the flavours to infuse, then add the soy sauce and mirin and simmer for a few minutes more.

Remove a little of the soup and place into a small bowl with the cornflour/cornstarch. Mix well so that you have a runny paste with no lumps. Add the cornflour/cornstarch mixture back to the pan gradually (you may not need it all), whisking all the time as you add it, until the soup starts to thicken slightly. Season with a little black pepper and taste for salt (the soup should already be salty from the soy sauce, but you can add a little more if you wish).

Beat the egg well, then tip into the piping/pastry bag fitted with a very fine nozzle/tip. Bring the soup to the boil so that it is very hot, then pipe the egg in a thin stream, so that it makes ribbons in the soup.

Serve straight away in bowls, dotting the surface of each portion with a teaspoon of caviar and a little gold leaf for extra shimmer.

CHAPTER 6

SOUP & A SANDWICH

GOULASH PEPPER SOUP WITH MEATBALL SUBS

Goulash is the national dish of Hungary and a very good dish it is, too! Traditionally made with beef, it has a gently paprika-spiced sauce finished with sour cream. This is my version – a (bell) pepper soup and a beef meatball sub on the side – delicious topped with sour cream, grated cheese and jalapeños.

1 onion, finely chopped
1 garlic clove, finely chopped
1 tablespoon olive oil
450-g/1-lb. jar of roasted red (bell) peppers preserved in brine
250 g/9 oz. passata/strained tomatoes
800 ml/generous 3¼ cups chicken or vegetable stock
2 teaspoons smoked paprika
a handful of torn fresh basil
4 tablespoons sour cream
salt and pepper

FOR THE MEATBALL SUBS
12 fresh meatballs
1 small onion, finely sliced
1 tablespoon olive oil
60 ml/¼ cup sherry
250 g/9 oz. passata/strained tomatoes
4 sub rolls
4 tablespoons grated Cheddar
a handful of fresh basil
6–8 jalapeño chilli/chile slices

SERVES 4

Start by preparing the meatball subs. Cook the meatballs following the packet instructions. For the sauce, fry the onion in the olive oil and sauté until soft and just starting to caramelize, stirring all the time. Add the sherry and simmer until it has reduced by half. Add the passata/strained tomatoes and simmer until the sauce thickens. Season with salt and pepper. Keep warm until you are ready to serve, or reheat before serving.

For the soup, add the onion and garlic to a saucepan with the olive oil and sauté over a gentle heat until soft and just turning light golden brown. Drain the roasted (bell) peppers and rinse them. Cut a few thin slices of the (bell) pepper and reserve for the garnish. Coarsely chop the remaining (bell) peppers, add to the pan and sauté for a few minutes. Add the passata/strained tomatoes, stock and smoked paprika and simmer for about 20 minutes.

Transfer to a blender or food processor and blitz until very smooth, or use a stick blender. Return to the pan and heat through. Season to taste with salt and pepper.

To finish the sandwiches, cut the sub rolls in half lengthways and add a layer of basil leaves. Place some of the warm meatballs in each roll and spoon over the warm meatball sauce. Sprinkle with grated cheese, which will melt in the heat of the sauce. Top with a few jalapeño slices.

Pour the soup into four bowls and garnish with the reserved thin strips of (bell) pepper, a little torn fresh basil and a sprinkling of pepper. Add a spoonful of sour cream or serve it on the side for diners to add to their own portion. Serve straight away with a meatball sub alongside each bowl of soup.

VEGETABLE SOUP WITH REUBEN SANDWICHES

This is comfort food at its best – a thick, wholesome vegetable soup served with classic New York Reuben sandwiches. I adore a Reuben sandwich – there is something so moreish about tangy horseradish mayo, sauerkraut and salt beef all warm with melting gooey cheese.

1 onion, finely chopped
1 stick/rib celery, chopped
1 garlic clove, finely chopped
1 tablespoon olive oil
1 leek, finely sliced
30 g/2 tablespoons butter
3 carrots, peeled and chopped
2 parsnips, peeled and chopped
800 ml/generous 3¼ cups vegetable stock
salt and pepper

FOR THE RUSSIAN DRESSING
2 egg yolks
1 teaspoon Dijon mustard
1 tablespoon white wine vinegar
200 ml/¾ cup mild olive oil
1 tablespoon horseradish
1 tablespoon tomato ketchup

FOR THE REUBEN SANDWICHES
8 slices rye bread
butter, for spreading
8–12 slices salt beef or pastrami
4 tablespoons prepared sauerkraut
8 slices Swiss cheese (such as Emmental)

sandwich press (optional)

SERVES 4

Begin by preparing the Russian dressing. Place the egg yolks, mustard and vinegar in a blender or food processor and blitz. With the blades on a slow speed, very slowly drizzle in the olive oil and whisk until the mayonnaise is thick. Fold through the horseradish and ketchup and season with salt and pepper. Store in the refrigerator until needed.

For the soup, add the onion, celery and garlic to a large saucepan with the olive oil and fry over a gentle heat until soft and the onion is translucent. Rinse the leek slices well to remove any dirt and then add to the pan with the butter. Cook gently for about 5 minutes until the leek has sweated down and is soft.

Add the chopped carrots and parsnips to the pan with the stock and simmer for about 15 minutes until the carrots and parsnips are soft. The actual cooking time will depend on the size of the vegetables. Once the vegetables are soft, carefully transfer to a blender or food processor and blitz until the soup is smooth, or use a stick blender. Return to the pan and keep warm until you are ready to serve.

For the sandwiches, lightly butter the outside of the rye bread, then turn over on a board and spread a layer of the Russian dressing over four of the slices. Top with the salt beef slices. Heat the sauerkraut to evaporate the liquid and then sprinkle a spoonful over the beef in each sandwich. Top with two slices of cheese and a further spoonful of dressing and then top each sandwich with the remaining buttered rye slices. Toast each sandwich in the sandwich press or in a griddle/ridged grill pan until warm and the cheese has melted.

Pour the soup into four bowls and add a sprinkling of pepper. Serve with the sandwiches on the side.

GARLIC MUSHROOM SOUP
WITH BRESAOLA-FILLED FOCACCIA

This soup is dedicated to my wonderful culinary mentor Giancarlo Caldesi, who taught me in his restaurant how to cook mushrooms so that they 'smell of the forest'. Cooked in butter with herbs and roasted garlic, these mushrooms will make your kitchen smell sensational.

30 g/2 tablespoons butter
1 tablespoon olive oil
1 shallot, finely chopped
250 g/9 oz. chestnut/cremini mushrooms, trimmed and cleaned with a brush or soft cloth
250 g/9 oz. button/white mushrooms, trimmed and cleaned with a brush or soft cloth
a sprig of fresh thyme
a sprig of fresh rosemary
1 teaspoon porcini mushroom paste (optional)
½ teaspoon finely grated lemon zest
75 ml/5 tablespoons sweet sherry
800 ml/generous 3¼ cups chicken or vegetable stock
salt and pepper

FOR THE ROASTED GARLIC PURÉE
2 whole garlic bulbs
1 tablespoon olive oil

FOR THE SANDWICHES
1 focaccia loaf
100 g/scant ½ cup cream cheese
a handful of rocket/arugula, leaves and flowers
50 g/2 oz. bresaola
shavings of Parmesan

SERVES 4

Begin by roasting the garlic. You can do this the day before and store in the refrigerator. Preheat the oven to 180°C (350°F) Gas 4. Place the whole garlic bulbs in a roasting pan and drizzle with the olive oil so the skin is lightly coated. Roast in the preheated oven for 30–40 minutes until the bulbs feel soft when you press them. Set aside to cool.

For the soup, place the butter and olive oil in a saucepan over a gentle heat and add the finely chopped shallot. Sauté for about 3–5 minutes until the shallot is soft and translucent. Add the mushrooms to the pan with the thyme and rosemary.

Cut the roasted garlic bulbs in half and squeeze out the soft garlic purée, making sure that you do not include any of the skin. Add one-quarter of the garlic purée to the saucepan (reserve the remainder for the sandwiches). Season with salt and pepper and, over a gentle heat, sauté the mushrooms for about 5 minutes until the mixture smells very earthy. Remove the thyme and rosemary sprigs.

Add the porcini paste to the pan with the lemon zest, then pour in the sherry and stock and simmer for 15 minutes. Remove a few whole mushrooms for the garnish, then blitz the soup to a smooth consistency in a blender or food processor, or use a stick blender. Season to taste and keep warm while you prepare the sandwiches.

To prepare the sandwiches, lightly warm the focaccia, then cut it into four wedges and slice each one in half horizontally. Spread the base of each sandwich with a generous layer of cream cheese. Top with some rocket/arugula leaves and flowers, then the bresaola and a few shavings of Parmesan. Spread the top of each sandwich with a little of the garlic purée and place on top to enclose the filling.

Pour the warm soup into bowls, garnish with the reserved whole mushrooms and serve with the sandwiches on the side.

CARROT & GINGER SOUP
WITH HUMMUS & PICKLED CARROT BAGUETTES

Although carrots may not make you see in the dark, they can certainly offer you a comforting 'pick-me-up' in the form of this earthy carrot and ginger soup. The soup is accompanied by a crusty baguette filled with delicious hummus and crunchy carrot pickle. If you like carrots, this will become one of your regular lunches.

1 tablespoon olive oil
1 small onion, finely chopped
1 tablespoon grated ginger
500 g/1 lb. 2 oz. carrots, peeled and chopped
1 litre/4 cups chicken or vegetable stock
25 g/1 oz. fresh coriander/ cilantro
juice of 1 large orange
salt and pepper

FOR THE CARROT PICKLE
1 carrot, peeled and trimmed
2 tablespoons white wine vinegar
2 teaspoons caster/granulated sugar
1 teaspoon cumin seeds

FOR THE SANDWICHES
1 baguette
150 g/5½ oz. hummus
a handful of spinach leaves
a handful of fresh coriander/ cilantro

SERVES 4

For the pickle, use a swivel peeler to make long strips of carrot. Place in a bowl with the vinegar and sugar. In a dry frying pan/skillet heat the cumin seeds until they start to pop, taking care that you do not burn them. Add to the bowl with a pinch of salt and stir so that the sugar and salt dissolve and the carrot strips are all coated in the pickling juices. Leave for about 1 hour to soak.

For the soup, heat the olive oil in a large saucepan and fry the chopped onion over a gentle heat until soft and translucent. Add the grated ginger and fry for a further 1–2 minutes. Add the chopped carrots to the pan with the stock, coriander/cilantro leaves and orange juice and simmer until the carrots are soft.

Place in a blender or food processor and blitz to a smooth purée, or use a stick blender. Return to the pan, season with salt and pepper and keep warm while you prepare the sandwiches.

Cut the baguette into four portions and slice each one in half horizontally. Fill with the hummus, spinach and coriander/cilantro leaves. Drain the pickling liquid from the carrots and add some of the carrot ribbons to each sandwich.

Pour the soup into four bowls and serve straight away with a sandwich on the side.

BROCCOLI SOUP
WITH BLUE CHEESE & PINE NUT CROISSANTS

Broccoli is one of the super vegetables that can really boost your immune system, so I like to make this soup when I am feeling under the weather – when blended it is an uplifting bright green colour. Broccoli goes really well with blue cheese and this soup is perfect served with warm stuffed croissants filled with tangy cheese and the crunch of toasted pine nuts.

1 tablespoon olive oil
1 onion, finely chopped
1 garlic clove, finely sliced
1 head of broccoli (about 300 g/10½ oz. in weight)
1 litre/4 cups chicken or vegetable stock
salt and pepper
4 tablespoons cream (optional)

FOR THE CROISSANTS
4 plain all-butter croissants
200 g/7 oz. gorgonzola dolce or other soft blue cheese
50 g/scant ½ cup pine nuts

SERVES 4

Heat the oil in a large saucepan over a gentle heat and fry the onion until soft and translucent. Add the garlic and fry until lightly golden brown. Cut the broccoli into small florets and discard the large stem. Add the florets to the pan with the stock and simmer for 10–15 minutes until the broccoli is just soft, but is still a vibrant green colour. If you overcook it, it will start to lose its colour.

Blitz the soup to a smooth consistency in a blender or food processor, or use a stick blender. Return to the pan, season with salt and pepper to taste and keep warm while you prepare the croissants.

Preheat the oven to 180°C (350°F) Gas 4.

Toast the pine nuts in a dry frying pan/skillet over a gentle heat until they are lightly golden brown.

Cut each of the croissants in half horizontally and place a slice or two of the cheese into each. Sprinkle the toasted pine nuts on top of the cheese. Replace the top of each croissant and wrap in a foil parcel. Bake in the preheated oven for about 5 minutes until the cheese starts to melt.

To serve, pour the soup into warm bowls, swirl in a spoonful of cream (if liked) and add a sprinkling of pepper. Serve with the warm croissants on the side.

MISO SOUP WITH SUSHI SANDWICHES

Miso is a warming Japanese broth – it takes very little time to prepare as it is made from a fermented soybean, rice or grain paste readily available in supermarkets. Each type of miso has its own flavour, so if you enjoy its earthy taste it is worth buying several types and blending them to find your perfect balance. Serve with a fun sushi 'sandwich'.

1 litre/4 cups dashi or vegetable stock
1 tablespoon yellow miso paste
1 tablespoon red miso paste
60 ml/¼ cup mirin (sweet rice wine)
2 spring onions/scallions, finely sliced
1 tablespoon soy sauce
200 g/7 oz. tofu, drained and cut into small cubes

FOR THE SUSHI 'SANDWICH'
125 g/⅔ cup sushi rice
1 tablespoon sushi vinegar
1 sheet of dried seaweed
2 large roasted red (bell) peppers in brine (such as Karyatis), drained

sushi mat

SERVES 4

Begin by preparing the sushi to serve with the soup. Cook the sushi rice following the packet instructions. (The brand I use comes as a boil-in-the-bag variety, which you cook for 25 minutes.) Once cooked, tip into a bowl and leave to cool. Stir in the sushi vinegar.

Cut the sheet of seaweed in half so that you have two pieces about 20 x 7.5 cm/8 x 3 inches and place one half on the sushi mat. Cover the seaweed with a thin layer of rice (using half of the rice), pressing it out with clean fingers. Open out the (bell) peppers so that they are in a single layer and place over the rice in a flat layer. Cover with the remainder of the rice, again pressing it out in a thin layer over the (bell) peppers. Cover with the second sheet of seaweed and fold over the sushi mat and press down so that the layer is compacted.

Remove the sushi mat and, using a very sharp knife, trim the sides of the sushi layer and then cut into triangles to look like sandwiches. Cover with clingfilm/plastic wrap and store in the refrigerator while you make the soup.

For the miso soup, place the dashi or stock in a large saucepan with the miso pastes and mirin and simmer over a gentle heat while stirring to dissolve the pastes.

Add the spring onions/scallions, soy sauce and tofu cubes and simmer for a few minutes more.

Pour into bowls and serve straight away with sushi 'sandwiches' on the side of each portion.

CHICKEN NOODLE BROTH
WITH LEMON TARRAGON CHICKEN ROLLS

This is a light broth, rich in chicken flavour with hints of aniseed from the tarragon. If you do not have time to boil the chicken, replace it with ready-cooked chicken and use a good-quality chicken stock instead.

1.35-kg/3-lb. whole chicken
2 large carrots, peeled and chopped
1 large leek, finely sliced
125 ml/½ cup sweet sherry
1 onion, chopped
2 tablespoons chopped fresh tarragon
2 teaspoons wholegrain mustard
2 spring onions/scallions, finely chopped
200 ml/generous ¾ cup white wine
125 g/4½ oz. thin dried egg noodles
salt and pepper

FOR THE ROLLS
1 tablespoon mayonnaise
2 tablespoons crème fraîche
2 teaspoons wholegrain mustard
1 tablespoon chopped fresh tarragon
grated zest of 1 lemon
4 soft white bread rolls

SERVES 4

Place the chicken in a large saucepan and add enough water to cover it. Add the carrots and leek to the pan with the sherry. Add the onion, season with salt and pepper and add 1 tablespoon of the chopped tarragon. Bring to the boil and then simmer the chicken gently for around 1 hour until the chicken is cooked and is starting to fall from the bone.

Carefully remove the chicken from the pan and set aside to cool. Strain the soup (discarding the vegetables, but reserving the stock) and skim any fat from the surface. Simmer the stock for a further 20 minutes until it has reduced by one-third to intensify the flavours, then let it cool. Chill the chicken and stock in the refrigerator.

Remove any fat that has set on top of the stock. Remove the chicken breasts from the cooled chicken and cut into slices. Return the chicken breast slices to the refrigerator for the sandwiches.

Remove the meat from the remainder of the chicken, discarding the bones and skin. Add the chicken to the stock in a saucepan and reheat, adding the mustard, spring onions/scallions, remaining tablespoon of tarragon and white wine. Heat and then taste the soup for seasoning adding more salt and pepper to your taste.

To prepare the rolls, whisk together the mayonnaise, crème fraîche, mustard and tarragon. Stir in the lemon zest and season to taste. Fold the dressing through the reserved chicken slices. Halve each roll and fill with a portion of the chicken and a sprinkling of pepper.

When you are ready to serve, add the noodles to the soup and simmer for around 3–5 minutes. Pour into bowls and serve straight away with the chicken rolls.

MOROCCAN CHICKPEA/GARBANZO BEAN SOUP WITH FALAFEL & HARISSA POCKETS

I love exploring the souks of Marrakech and admiring the amazing spice towers, the air filled with delicious aromas. Moroccan food is so flavoursome with hints of cinnamon and citrus, as well as fiery heat. My favourite harissa is made with rose petals (Belazu make a wonderful one), but if you cannot find it, substitute regular harissa paste instead.

15 g/1 tablespoon butter
1 tablespoon olive oil
3 shallots, finely chopped
1 garlic clove, finely sliced
1 teaspoon black onion/nigella seeds
1 teaspoon ground cinnamon
freshly squeezed juice of 2 lemons
1 teaspoon rose harissa
2 x 400-g/14-oz. cans chickpeas/garbanzo beans, drained
80 g/½ cup soft dried apricots
1 litre/4 cups chicken or vegetable stock
black pepper
fennel fronds, to garnish (optional)

FOR THE FALAFEL POCKETS
1 teaspoon rose harissa
200 g/1 cup Greek yogurt
12 ready-made falafels
4 wholemeal pitta pockets
a few handfuls of mixed soft salad leaves

SERVES 4

For the soup, heat the butter and oil in a saucepan over a gentle heat and fry the shallots until soft and translucent. Add the garlic and fry until lightly golden brown. Add the black onion/nigella seeds and cinnamon and fry for a minute to heat the spices, stirring all the time. Add the lemon juice, harissa, chickpeas/garbanzo beans, apricots and stock to the pan and simmer for about 20 minutes.

Pour the soup into a blender or food processor and blitz until smooth, or use a stick blender. Return to the pan and keep warm.

To make the harissa yogurt dressing for the falafel pockets, fold the harissa into the Greek yogurt and season with salt and pepper to your taste. Cover and store in the refrigerator until you are ready to serve.

When ready to serve, cook the falafel according to the packet instructions. Warm the pitta breads under the grill/broiler and then cut them open. Fill each with salad leaves and falafel and top with a drizzle of the harissa yogurt dressing.

Pour the soup into four bowls and top with chopped fennel fronds, if using, and some freshly ground black pepper. Serve straight away with the falafel pockets on the side.

SWEET RED PEPPER, FENNEL & OUZO SOUP
WITH PRAWN/SHRIMP SAGANAKI PITTAS

On a trip to Cyprus our hotel served prawn saganaki and I loved it so much that I ordered it almost every night! It had a delicious aniseed flavour as it was cooked with ouzo and was sprinkled with salty feta cheese. It is the inspiration for this deliciously summery soup.

2 onions, finely sliced
2 garlic cloves, finely sliced
1–2 tablespoons olive oil, plus extra to drizzle
1 bulb of fennel, trimmed
3 sweet red (bell) peppers, deseeded and chopped
75 ml/5 tablespoons ouzo
300 g/10½ oz. passata/strained tomatoes
600 ml/2½ cups chicken or vegetable stock
salt and pepper

FOR THE PITTAS
200 g/7 oz. feta cheese
60 ml/¼ cup ouzo
200 g/7 oz. passata/strained tomatoes
1 tablespoon chopped fresh mint
225 g/8 oz. raw prawns/shrimp, shells removed
1 tablespoon olive oil
4 white pitta pockets

SERVES 4

In a saucepan, sauté the onions and garlic in 1 tablespoon of the olive oil over a gentle heat until softened and the onions start to caramelize. Stir all the time to ensure they do not burn. Put half of the onions and garlic in an ovenproof dish and set aside.

Chop most of the fennel, reserving a piece to peel into ribbons for the garnish as well as any fronds, and add to the onions with the (bell) peppers and a little more olive oil if needed. Sauté until the (bell) peppers and fennel soften, stirring frequently. Add the ouzo and cook for 1 minute. Add the passata/strained tomatoes and stock and season with salt and pepper. Simmer for about 15–20 minutes.

Pour the soup into a blender or food processor and blitz until very smooth, or use a stick blender. Season to taste. Keep warm while you prepare the pittas.

Preheat the oven to 180°C (350°F) Gas 4.

For the saganaki sauce, crumble the feta on top of the reserved onions and garlic in the ovenproof dish. Pour over the ouzo and the passata/strained tomatoes. Sprinkle with the mint and bake in the preheated oven for 15–20 minutes until the cheese is soft.

Meanwhile, in a hot frying pan/skillet or wok, pan fry the prawns/shrimp in the olive oil for 3–5 minutes until the prawns/shrimp have turned a deep pink colour and are slightly golden around the edges.

Place a large spoonful of the saganaki sauce into each pitta and fill with the prawns/shrimp.

Pour the soup into four bowls. Using a swivel vegetable peeler, peel thin ribbons of the reserved fennel and use to garnish the soup, along with any fennel fronds. Drizzle with a little extra olive oil and serve straight away with the filled pittas.

THAI HOT & SPICY COCONUT SOUP
WITH CHICKEN SATAY FLATBREADS

This soup is hot and spicy with a real kick. Thai 'tom yum' paste is a readily available ingredient and adds real flavour here. You'll need to use a soft dark brown sugar for this recipe and try to find Thai basil for authenticity. The nutty chicken satay flatbread is the perfect accompaniment.

1 tablespoon coconut oil
1 tablespoon tom yum paste
2 tablespoons dark soy sauce
2 tablespoons fish sauce
1 tablespoon soft dark brown sugar
freshly squeezed juice of 3 limes
2 very large tomatoes
200 ml/¾ cup coconut milk
250 g/9 oz. chestnut/cremini mushrooms
1 red chilli/chile, finely sliced
2 spring onions/scallions, finely sliced
a handful of Thai basil
a handful of coriander/cilantro
225 g/8 oz. raw/uncooked king prawns/jumbo shrimp
black pepper

FOR THE SATAY SAUCE
125 ml/½ cup coconut milk
2 tablespoons peanut butter
freshly squeezed juice of 1 lime
1 tablespoon fish sauce
1 tablespoon soy sauce
1 tablespoon brown sugar
½ tablespoon tamarind paste

FOR THE FLATBREADS
2 skinless chicken breasts
1 tablespoon olive oil
4 flatbreads
1 tablespoon salted peanuts, roughly chopped
a handful of chopped fresh coriander/cilantro

SERVES 4

For the soup, heat the coconut oil in a large saucepan, add the tom yum paste and fry over a gentle heat quickly. Add 1 litre/4 cups of water to the pan together with the soy sauce, fish sauce, sugar and lime juice. Cut the tomatoes into slim wedges and add to the pan, then pour in the coconut milk. Simmer until warm.

Clean and trim the mushrooms, cut them in half and add to the pan, then simmer until they are soft. Add the sliced chilli/chile and spring onions/scallions, Thai basil and coriander/cilantro.

Just before you are ready to serve the soup, cut a slit along the back of each prawn/shrimp (do not cut all the way through – you just want to cut a slit deep enough so that the prawns/shrimp curl up when they are cooked), discard the black veins and add the prawns/shrimp to the pan. Simmer for a few minutes until the prawns/shrimp are pink and cooked through. Season with a little black pepper if you wish (there should be sufficient salt from the fish sauce and soy sauce).

For the flatbreads, begin by preparing the satay sauce. Place the coconut milk in a saucepan with the peanut butter and whisk over a gentle heat until smooth. Add the lime juice, fish sauce, soy sauce, sugar and tamarind paste and whisk until everything is incorporated. Set aside.

Chop the chicken into small pieces and fry in a pan with the oil for 6–8 minutes until lightly golden brown and cooked through. Stir in the satay sauce and simmer gently for a few minutes. Warm the flatbreads.

To serve, pour the soup into bowls. Place the flatbreads onto plates and top each with a generous spoonful of the satay chicken. Sprinkle over the peanuts and coriander/cilantro. Season with black pepper and serve.

Sheffield
De Luxe Stainless
England

BUTTERNUT SQUASH SOUP
WITH THANKSGIVING PRETZEL SANDWICHES

After all the festivities of Thanksgiving, there are often some slices of turkey and some cranberry sauce left over. I love to serve these in giant soft pretzel sandwiches, similar to those I have enjoyed on trips to Bavaria, but if you can't find pretzels, thick-cut slices of white bread are equally delicious. Using seasonal butternut squash, this spicy soup makes a pleasant change the day after Thanksgiving.

2 onions, finely chopped
1 tablespoon olive oil
1 teaspoon garam masala
1 tablespoon black onion/ nigella seeds
½ teaspoon ground cinnamon
a pinch of cayenne pepper
900 g/2 lb. butternut squash, peeled, deseeded and cut into chunks
800 ml/generous 3¼ cups chicken or vegetable stock
black pepper

FOR THE PRETZELS
4 large soft pretzels
2–3 spoonfuls mayonnaise
4 large slices cooked turkey
4 tablespoons cranberry sauce
4 slices Swiss cheese

SERVES 4

Place the onions in a large saucepan with the oil and cook over a gentle heat until the onions are soft and translucent.

Add the garam masala, black onion/nigella seeds, cinnamon and cayenne pepper. If you do not like spicy soup, then omit the cayenne pepper. Fry for a few minutes further to allow the spices to heat.

Add the squash to the pan and cook for a few minutes, then add the stock and simmer for about 30 minutes until the squash is soft.

Pour the soup into the blender or food processor and blitz until smooth, or use a stick blender. Keep warm until you are ready to serve.

For the sandwiches, carefully slice each pretzel in half horizontally and spread each half with a little mayonnaise. Place a slice of turkey on each base and top with some cranberry sauce. Add a slice of Swiss cheese and cover each with a pretzel top. (If you wish, you can toast the pretzels until the cheese starts to melt.)

Pour the soup into warm bowls, sprinkle with freshly ground black pepper and serve straight away with the sandwiches on the side.

WHITE BEAN & PANCETTA SOUP
WITH ROASTED VEGETABLE PICNIC LOAVES

This soup transports me to the Tuscan hills where cannellini bean soup is popular lunchtime fare. Adding thyme and pancetta gives it a wonderfully smoky taste. The accompanying stuffed mini picnic loaves are perfect for summer eating, packed with delicious antipasti-style roasted (bell) peppers and aubergines/eggplants.

1 small white onion, finely chopped
1 tablespoon olive oil
200 g/7 oz. pancetta cubes
1 garlic clove, finely chopped
4 sprigs of fresh thyme
400-g/14-oz. can cannellini beans, drained and rinsed
125 ml/½ cup Marsala wine
800 ml/generous 3¼ cups chicken stock
salt and pepper

FOR THE PICNIC LOAVES
2 aubergines/eggplants
olive oil, to drizzle
freshly squeezed juice of 1 lemon
4 small ciabatta rolls
4 flame-roasted (bell) peppers, preserved in brine, rinsed and patted dry on paper towels
a handful of baby spinach leaves

SERVES 4

Preheat the oven to 180°C (350°F) Gas 4.

Begin by preparing the aubergines/eggplants for the picnic loaves. Trim the ends away and cut them into slices about 1 cm/⅜ inch thick. Place in a roasting pan, drizzle generously with olive oil and roast for 30 minutes until the aubergines/eggplants are golden brown. Leave to cool in the roasting oil, then squeeze over the lemon juice and store in the refrigerator until needed.

For the soup, fry the onion in the olive oil in a saucepan over a gentle heat until it is soft and translucent. Add the pancetta, garlic and sprigs of thyme to the pan and fry until the pancetta is cooked and starts to turn slightly golden brown. Stir all the time to make sure that it does not burn. Add the beans to the pan and cook for 5 minutes so that the beans absorb the flavours of the oil.

Remove two generous spoonfuls of the beans and pancetta and place in a small bowl. Remove the thyme from the pan, strip the leaves from the stalks and add to the bowl. Toss in a little olive oil and set aside for the garnish.

Add the Marsala wine and the chicken stock to the saucepan and simmer for 15 minutes, or longer if you wish. Season with salt and pepper, if needed, but I generally find the soup has enough salt from the pancetta. Blitz in a blender or food processor to a smooth purée, or use a stick blender. Keep warm while you prepare the loaves.

Cut the tops off the rolls and pull out the centre of the bread (you can blitz into crumbs and freeze). Line the bottom of each loaf with a few spinach leaves, then layer with aubergine/eggplant and (bell) peppers until the holes are full. Top with the lids.

Pour the soup into four bowls and garnish with the reserved beans, pancetta and thyme. Serve with the loaves on the side.

CHAPTER 7
BREADS

SODA BREAD

Soda bread is traditionally from Ireland and is very quick and easy to prepare. It contains no yeast as the recipe uses bicarbonate of soda/baking soda to make it rise. It is great to serve with soups. Cutting the cross on top of the loaf is important as it allows it to cook all the way through.

250 g/2 cups plain/all-purpose flour, plus extra for dusting
250 g/2 cups wholemeal/ wholewheat flour
1 teaspoon bicarbonate of soda/ baking soda
1 teaspoon salt
420 ml/scant 1¾ cups buttermilk or milk soured with a squeeze of lemon juice

a baking sheet, lined with parchment paper

MAKES 1 LOAF

Preheat the oven to 200°C (400°F) Gas 6.

In a large bowl, mix together the two types of flour, bicarbonate of soda/baking soda and salt. Add the buttermilk and mix until a sticky dough forms.

Lightly flour a work surface and tip the dough onto it. Gently roll and fold the dough a few times to bring the mixture together. Do not be tempted to knead. Shape the dough into a ball. Flatten the ball gently with floured hands. Use a sharp knife to score the dough with a deep cross, dividing it into quarters. Dust the bread with the extra plain/ all-purpose flour.

Place the dough onto the prepared baking sheet and bake in the preheated oven for 30 minutes. The loaf should be golden-brown, crusty on top and make a hollow sound when tapped on the bottom. Leave to cool on a wire rack before slicing.

The loaf is best eaten on the day you make it, but can be reheated in the oven the following day, or sliced and frozen.

BUTTERMILK BISCUITS

Fear not those of you to whom a 'biscuit' means a sweet cookie, as these are my version of classic American biscuits, which are warm scones – a perfect accompaniment for soup. These are best eaten on the day they are made.

225 g/1¾ cups self-raising/ self-rising flour, sifted
¼ teaspoon salt
¼ teaspoon pepper
½ teaspoon baking powder
60 g/½ stick salted butter, chilled and cubed
60 g/⅔ cup grated Cheddar, plus extra for sprinkling (optional)
1 heaped teaspoon wholegrain mustard
125 ml/½ cup buttermilk, plus extra if needed
1 egg, beaten

6-cm/5½-inch round cutter
large baking sheet, greased and lined

SERVES 4

Preheat the oven to 180°C (350°F) Gas 4.

Place the flour, salt, pepper and baking powder in a large mixing bowl. Rub the chilled butter into the flour lightly with your fingertips until it resembles fine breadcrumbs. Add the grated cheese, mustard and buttermilk and mix to form a soft dough. Add a little more buttermilk or regular milk if the mixture is too dry.

On a lightly floured surface, gently roll out the dough to 2.5 cm/1 in. thickness and cut out the biscuits with the 6-cm/5½-in. cutter.

Place the biscuits on the baking sheet so that they are almost touching. Brush the tops with the beaten egg and sprinkle with a little extra grated cheese, if liked.

Bake in the preheated oven for 25–30 minutes until golden brown and the biscuits sound hollow when you tap them. Leave on the baking sheet for 5 minutes, then transfer to a rack to cool.

CORNBREAD MUFFINS

These savoury muffins are ideal served with soup, especially with something like the Smoky Black Bean Soup (see page 59) or the Prawn/ Shrimp Gumbo Soup (see page 56).

150 g/1 cup fine cornmeal/ polenta
30 g/4 tablespoons self-raising/ self-rising flour
1 teaspoon bicarbonate of soda/ baking soda
¼ teaspoon hot paprika
300 ml/1¾ cups buttermilk
20 g/1 tablespoon soft butter
1 egg
165 g/1 cup sweetcorn/corn kernels
salt and pepper

12-hole muffin pan, greased

SERVES 4

Preheat the oven to 190°C (375°F) Gas 5.

Place the cornmeal (or fine polenta), flour, bicarbonate of soda/baking soda, paprika, buttermilk, butter and egg in a mixing bowl and whisk together until you have a smooth thick batter. Fold in the sweetcorn/ corn kernels and season with salt and pepper.

Divide the cornbread mixture between eight of the holes of the greased muffin pan. (If you prefer you can line the muffin pan with paper cases rather than greasing.)

Bake in the preheated oven for 30–35 minutes, until the muffins are golden brown on top. Remove from the oven and serve warm.

GLUTEN-FREE TOPPED CORNBREAD

This gluten-free cornbread with a spicy melted cheese topping makes a satisfying snack on its own, but it is also the perfect partner to a bowl of soup, especially when served warm from the oven.

for UK bakers, 100 g gluten-free self-raising flour plus 1 teaspoon baking powder, OR for US bakers, ¾ cup gluten-free all-purpose flour plus 2 teaspoons baking powder and ½ teaspoon xanthan gum
300 g/2 cups fine cornmeal/polenta
2 teaspoons bicarbonate of soda/baking soda
4 tablespoons chopped fresh coriander/cilantro
grated zest of 1 lime
3 spring onions/scallions, finely chopped
500 ml/2 cups buttermilk
50 g/3½ tablespoons butter, melted and cooled
3 eggs
salt and pepper

FOR THE TOPPING
2–3 red chillies/chiles, to taste, finely sliced
1 tablespoon olive oil
1 tablespoon finely chopped coriander/cilantro
2 teaspoons caster/granulated sugar
100 g/1 cup grated Cheddar

30 x 20-cm/12 x 8-inch baking pan, greased and lined with baking parchment

MAKES 1 LARGE LOAF

Begin by preparing the topping. Fry the chillies/chiles in a saucepan with the olive oil over a gentle heat until soft. Season with salt and pepper, add the chopped coriander/cilantro and cook for a few minutes more. Sprinkle over the sugar and cook for a further minute until the chillies/chiles start to caramelize, then leave to cool.

Preheat the oven to 190°C (375°F) Gas 5.

Sift the flour and baking powder (plus xanthan gum, if using) into a large mixing bowl and stir in the cornmeal (or fine polenta), bicarbonate of soda/baking soda, coriander/cilantro, lime zest and spring onions/scallions.

In a separate bowl, whisk together the buttermilk, melted butter and eggs and season with salt and pepper. Add this to the dry ingredients and mix everything together.

Pour the mixture into the prepared baking pan and spread level using a spatula. Sprinkle the grated cheese over the top of the batter, then evenly distribute the chillies/chiles. Bake in the preheated oven for about 30–35 minutes until the loaf is golden brown on top.

The bread is best served warm on the day it is made.

SAVOURY MUFFINS

These savoury muffins, packed with cheese, sweetcorn/corn kernels and chilli/chile make a delicious accompaniment to soup. You can replace the sweetcorn/corn kernels with other things to add texture and flavour, such as bacon pieces or sun-dried tomatoes, if you prefer.

350 g/2⅔ cups self-raising/rising flour, sifted
1 teaspoon baking powder
1 teaspoon bicarbonate of soda/baking soda
150 g/5½ oz. canned sweetcorn/corn kernels, drained
200 g/2½ cups grated Cheddar
50 g/¾ cup grated Parmesan
1 red chilli/chile, deseeded and finely chopped
200 ml/¾ cup milk
150 g/⅔ cup sour cream
100 g/7 tablespoons butter, melted
2 eggs
1 heaped teaspoon Dijon mustard
2 heaped teaspoons caster/granulated sugar
salt and pepper
a few drops of Worcestershire sauce

12-hole muffin pan, lined with muffin cases

MAKES 12

Preheat the oven to 180°C (350°F) Gas 4.

Place the flour, baking powder and bicarbonate of soda/baking soda in a large mixing bowl and stir well so that everything is mixed. Add the sweetcorn/corn kernels, three-quarters of the grated Cheddar and all of the Parmesan. Stir in together with the finely chopped chilli/chile.

In a separate bowl, whisk together the milk, soured cream, melted butter, eggs, mustard and sugar and season with salt and pepper. Pour the milk mixture into the bowl containing the dry ingredients and fold in with a whisk. The batter should be thick and slightly lumpy.

Divide the mixture between the muffin cases and bake in the preheated oven for 15–20 minutes until the muffins are golden brown and firm to the touch. About 5 minutes before the end of cooking, sprinkle the tops of the muffins with the remaining grated Cheddar and a dash of Worcestershire sauce. The muffins can be served warm or cold.

PARMESAN POPOVERS

When my brother moved to America, he was so happy to learn that our favourite roast dinner treat in England (Yorkshire pudding) is eaten alongside many other dishes as the ever-popular popover! Popovers are cooked in deep pans so that they have an almost cone shape and can be flavoured with cheese or fresh herbs, or just be kept plain if you wish. They are a great accompaniment to any soup, in place of a bread roll. Traditionally you need a popover pan to make these, but if you don't have one, then individual dariole moulds placed on a baking sheet or a deep muffin tray/pan works just as well.

4 eggs
300 g/2¼ cups plain/all-purpose flour, sifted
375 ml/1½ cups plus 1 tablespoon milk
50 g/¾ cup grated Parmesan
salt and pepper
melted butter and olive oil, for greasing

12-hole muffin tin/popover pan or 12 individual dariole moulds

MAKES 12

Beat the eggs in a bowl, then add the flour and whisk in until you have a thick paste. Add the milk gradually, whisking hard to ensure there are no lumps. Season with salt and pepper and fold in the Parmesan, then leave to rest for about 30 minutes, covered.

Preheat the oven to 200°C (400°F) Gas 6.

Grease the popover pan or dariole moulds well with melted butter and olive oil, making sure that there is a little pool of fat in the bottom of each pan or mould. Place the pans in the oven to heat them for about 5 minutes. You want the oil and butter to be hot before pouring in the batter to get the best rise.

Whisk the batter again then pour it into each of the moulds until they are about two-thirds full. Bake in the preheated oven for about 30–35 minutes until they are risen and golden brown. If they start to brown too much, turn the oven temperature down towards the end of baking. Serve warm on the day they are made.

INDEX

ACKNOWLEDGEMENTS

With all my thanks to the amazing team at Ryland Peters & Small, as always, for publishing such a beautiful and creative book, particularly to Editorial Director Julia Charles, my dearest friend, for commissioning the book and allowing me to share with you my love of soups. A particular thank you to Creative Director Leslie Harrington and Designer Paul Stradling for the wonderful design; to Photographer Alex Luck, thank you so much for the beautiful new images, and to Octavia Squire and Ellie Tarn for food styling, and Luis Peral for sourcing such lovely props – you captured the essence of each soup in a perfect way – you are such an amazing team and I am so lucky to have you. And finally to Patricia Harrington and Gordana Simakovic for their skillful book production.

Heather and Elly at HHB, thank you for all your valued help and support over the many years we have worked together.

To the wonderful BARAKURA ENGLISH GARDEN in Chino, Japan and particularly the Yamada Family and Yamazaki San, thank you for introducing me to Japanese cuisine and flavours which inspired some of the recipes in this book.

To my husband John and Katie, my Mum and Dad, Liz and Mike, Gareth and Amy, Lucy and David, Maren, Alison, Adrienne, Bill and Beryl, Maggie, Debs, Taffy and Charlotte, Miles, Jess, Josh and Rosie – who ate more bowls of soup than you can imagine – thank you all for always being there and eating life with a big spoon – love you all x

PHOTOGRAPHY CREDITS

All photography by **Alex Luck** with the exception of the following pages:

Steve Painter
Pages 18, 21, 22, 25, 26, 58, 61, 64, 67, 68, 90, 93, 94, 114, 117, 138, 141, 142, 145, 146, 149, 150, 153, 154, 157, 158.

William Reavell
Pages 164, 168.